MW00851586

STALIN'S

FORGOTTEN ZION

The publisher gratefully acknowledges the contribution provided by the General Endowment Fund, which is supported by generous gifts from the members of the Associates of the University of California Press.

STALIN'S FORGOTTEN ZION

ROBERT WEINBERG

With an Introduction by
ZVI GITELMAN

Photographs edited by
BRADLEY BERMAN

Birobidzhan and the Making of a Soviet Jewish Homeland

AN ILLUSTRATED HISTORY, 1928–1996

University of California Press / Berkeley / Los Angeles / London
Judah L. Magnes Museum / Berkeley

Illustration, page xi: The June 1934 cover of
ICOR: Birobidzhan Souvenir, by William
Gropper, celebrating the establishment of the
Jewish Autonomous Region (J.A.R.).

University of California Press
Berkeley and Los Angeles, California

University of California Press, Ltd.
London, England

© 1998 by
The Regents of the University of California

Library of Congress
Cataloging-in-Publication Data

Weinberg, Robert.
    Stalin's forgotten Zion : Birobidzhan and the
making of a Soviet Jewish homeland : an illustrated history, 1928–1996 / Robert Weinberg ;
with an introduction by Zvi Gitelman ; photographs edited by Bradley Berman.
        p.   cm.
    Includes bibliographical references and index.
ISBN 0-520-20989-3 (cloth : alk. paper). —
ISBN 0-520-20990-7 (pbk. : alk. paper)
    1. Jews—Russia—Evreĭskaia avtonomnaia
oblast'—History.   2. Jews—Russia—
Birobidzhan—History.   3. Evreĭskaia
avtonomnaia oblast' (Russia)—History.
4. Birobidzhan (Russia)—History.
5. Russia—Ethnic relations. I. Title.
DS135.R93E989   1998
957'.7—dc21   97-5052
                                                 CIP
                                                 r97

Printed in the United States of America
9 8 7 6 5 4 3 2 1

The paper used in this publication meets the
minimum requirements of American National
Standard for Information Sciences—Perm-
anence of Paper for Printed Library Materials,
ANSI Z39.48-1984. ∞

CONTENTS

This book would not have been
possible without the inspiration and commitment
of the leadership and staff of the
Historical Museum of the Jewish Autonomous Region.

ACKNOWLEDGMENTS

This book accompanies an exhibition organized by the Judah L. Magnes Museum of Berkeley, California, in conjunction with the State Historical Museum of the Jewish Autonomous Region (J.A.R.) in Russia. In 1993 Tatiana Kosvintseva, director of the State Historical Museum of the J.A.R., invited the Magnes Museum to coproduce a show about the history of the region. Seymour Fromer, director of the Magnes Museum, and then traveling exhibitions curator Bradley Berman were intrigued by Kosvintseva's offer. They contacted me to see whether I would join the (ad)venture of putting together such an exhibit.

My interest in the J.A.R., popularly known as Birobidzhan, the region's capital city, was piqued in 1982 when I was a graduate student living in the main building of Moscow State University. One morning, as I was exiting the building on the way to the library, I did a double take when I noticed a newspaper printed with the Hebrew alphabet for sale at a kiosk. On closer examination I realized that the newspaper was the *Birobidzhaner shtern* (The Birobidzhan star), the Yiddish daily from Birobidzhan, the purported national territory of Soviet Jewry. I bought a copy of the paper and remembered to check the kiosk for the next eight months for future issues. Unfortunately, my diligence was not rewarded very often, since delivery of the *Birobidzhaner shtern* was irregular. Nonetheless, I made a mental note to turn my attention to Birobidzhan after I finished my project on Odessa during the Revolution of 1905. That opportunity came in the early 1990s, when I began to explore the history of Birobidzhan in earnest. In March 1992 I spent a month in Birobidzhan, working in the library and archives and learning as much as I could about the past and present of the Soviet Zion.

I jumped at the opportunity to work with the Magnes Museum and encouraged Seymour and Brad to pursue outside funding to finance a trip to Birobidzhan so we could ascertain the feasibility of such an exhibition. In October 1994 Brad and I, accompanied by Dale Archibald of the Oregon Historical Society and Nikolai Borodulin, a native of Birobidzhan working at the YIVO Institute for Jewish Research in New York, spent ten days as guests of the State Historical Museum of the J.A.R. and the Ministry of Culture of the J.A.R. We found a treasure trove of rare photographs and documents, vintage film footage, and other priceless artifacts that convinced us of the artistic and scholarly merit of exhibiting the material. We returned home confident that we had a mission to bring the story of Birobidzhan to as many people as possible.

Working on the exhibition and book has been a labor of love, made all the easier by the people who have helped at various stages of the project. I would like to thank Seymour Fromer, who had the vision to pursue the project from the start and offered the resources and support of the Magnes Museum to Brad and me. This exhibition would not have reached fruition had it not been for Seymour's initial excitement and his subsequent encouragement and guidance. I also want to thank Tatiana Kosvintseva and her husband, Boris Kosvintsev, for their assistance in helping us to collect many of the materials shown in the exhibition and then in arranging for their transport to the United States. Along with Misha Waiman, director of the Jewish Cultural Center in Birobidzhan who died soon after our visit in 1994, Tanya and Boris were warm and generous hosts during our trip to the J.A.R., and they made our stay hospitable and rewarding. Thanks are also due to Larissa Vilichinska for her services as translator.

A special debt of gratitude is owed Nikolai Borodulin, whom I first met during my 1992 trip to Birobidzhan. We kept up our friendship after his arrival in the United States in the fall of 1993. Kolya's extensive knowledge of the history of the J.A.R. and his expert research skills have enabled him to unearth a wealth of valuable materials in both the United States and Birobidzhan. In addition, he saved the day on more than one occasion with his services as a translator of Yiddish materials. It is no exaggeration to say that Kolya's contributions have enriched the project, and his invaluable assistance deserves special mention.

My deepest debt of gratitude goes to my collaborator, Brad Berman, who produced the exhibition from start to finish. In addition to his numerous tasks as project director, he raised funds and organized two trips to the J.A.R. Perhaps most important was his ability to establish and maintain a close working relationship with our colleagues in Birobidzhan, without which this project would never have materialized. Despite a harrowing encounter with Russian customs officials during his solo trip to the J.A.R. in May 1996, Brad's success in acquiring crucial photographs and documents underscores his dedication to the project. As a result of his efforts, audiences in the United States will experience the history of the J.A.R. through a national touring exhibition, in which artifacts from the region will be seen for the first time outside the Russian Far East. I applaud his hard work, determination, and commitment and thank him especially for his good nature, calm demeanor, and optimism. He never lost faith in what we were doing and made working on the project a rewarding experience. It has been a genuine pleasure collaborating with Brad, and the bonds we formed over the past several years have grown into what promises to be a long-lasting friendship.

I also owe a debt of scholarly thanks to the following specialists who took time from their own very busy schedules to read and comment on various drafts of the exhibition proposal and this book: Abraham Ascher, Laurie Bernstein, Zvi Gitelman, Bruce Grant, George Mosse, Alexander Orbach, Emilie Passow, Yuri Slezkine, and Steve Zipperstein. Their insightful criticisms saved me from numerous errors and prompted me to reformulate and rethink parts of my presentation and analysis. Needless to say, they are not responsible for any of the shortcomings still found in the exhibition or this book.

In addition, let me express my sincere thanks to Doug Abrams Arava and the staff at the University of California Press for their professionalism and expert handling of transforming the exhibition into book form. Elizabeth Levinsky of the Magnes Museum also provided invaluable translating services for Brad; in addition, she helped Brad host Tanya and Boris when they spent a week in Berkeley as guests of the Magnes Museum. Special thanks also to the exhibition designer, Gordon Chun, and the project consultant, Hal Fisher.

Finally, the exhibition and my research on the J.A.R. would not have been possible without the generous financial assistance provided by the following institutions: American Philosophical Society, Fulbright-Hays Faculty Research Abroad Program, Hoover Institution (U.S. Department of State's Soviet–Eastern European Research and Training Act of 1983, Title VIII Program), International Research and Exchanges Board, Memorial Foundation for Jewish Culture, Ministry of Culture of the Jewish Autonomous Region, National Endowment for the Humanities, San Francisco Jewish Community Endowment Fund, Social Science Research Council, Swarthmore College, and Trust for Mutual Understanding. The staffs at the YIVO Institute for Jewish Research and the National Center for Jewish Film at Brandeis University also provided invaluable research. I know that I speak on behalf of all the people involved in the project when I thank the granting institutions for the faith they placed in us.

Images from an album made in
the mid-1930s by the authorities
of the J.A.R. who wanted to
show satisfied and happy
settlers.

INTRODUCTION

ZVI GITELMAN

The project to settle Jews in Birobidzhan was one of the most exotic and controversial attempts to solve what was perceived as a "Jewish problem" in the Russian Empire and its successor state, the Soviet Union. That such a problem existed was a commonplace. But people had radically different opinions as to its cause. Some believed that the problem lay in the intrinsic characteristics of the Jewish people. After all, they had killed Christ and were inherently untrustworthy and evil; whatever disadvantages they suffered were justified punishments for the deicide and the subsequent evils they had brought to the world. Others saw the problem as stemming from the artificially imposed and unfortunate position of Jews in the social and economic structures of the country. Still others believed that the "Jewish problem" was really the problem of the Russian and Soviet states, which imposed disabilities on Jews. Whatever one's persuasion, at the beginning of the twentieth century, the "Jewish problem" drew the attention of Jews and non-Jews alike.

The Russian Empire had the largest Jewish population in the world. The census of 1897 enumerated 5,215,800 Jews, but between 1881 and 1914 nearly two million emigrated, seeking better economic opportunities and escaping persecution. The tsars had barred Jews from living in their empire until the late eighteenth century, when they annexed eastern Poland with its large Jewish population. They did not want the Jews, but they coveted the territories the Jews inhabited. In an era in which genocide and "ethnic cleansing" were not yet widely practiced, the tsars hit on the device of annexing the territories but confining the Jews in them in what came to be known as the "Pale of Settlement" (see map on p. 17). Over 90 percent of the Jews were confined to the Pale, with only the privileged—merchants of the first and second "guilds" (that is, the wealthy), people with highly specialized skills, and long-term soldiers—allowed to live outside the fifteen western provinces of the empire which made up the Pale.

All Jews, irrespective of their residence, were subject to a second kind of restriction, the *numerus clausus,* a quota system that limited severely the number of Jews who could be admitted to secondary and higher educational institutions and to the professions. Yet, as Robert Weinberg points out in this book, tsarist (and Soviet) policies were contradictory, for along with these restrictions, the authorities attempted to assimilate the Jews by driving them into state schools, where they would be weaned from their religious and ethnic loyalties. Some Jews saw the latter policy as a way of "emancipating" the Jews and gaining cultural and, eventually, political and legal equality. Other Jews regarded the offer of general education as a seductive snare designed to lead to mass conversion to Christianity and the destruction of the Jewish people by cultural means.

Jews were also subjected to a variety of political and economic restrictions. They could not be civil servants or military officers, or engage in commerce outside the Pale except with special permits, and few were allowed to own land. This was crucial because agriculture was the source of income of about 80 percent of the empire's population.[1] These restrictions condemned most Jews to poverty and desperation. Jews were also victimized by pogroms (riots), which the government did little to prevent and which led to considerable loss of property and lives. After a wave of pogroms broke out in the southern parts of the empire in 1881, following the assassination of Tsar Alexander II for which Jews were blamed, mass emigration began.[2]

In the nineteenth century Jews and others devised a number of solutions to the "Jewish problem." Some blamed the Jewish situation mainly on the Jews themselves and pointed to their physical and cultural isolation from the rest of the population as the source of their troubles. The obvious remedy was to promote Jewish integration into the larger society and its cultures, provided that society would accept them. When some of the tsars seemed to move toward such reforms, the advocates of assimilation eagerly seized on this and urged Jews to melt into Russian society. A more moderate stance was adopted by the "enlighteners" (*maskilim*) who, unlike their West European counterparts, did not advocate abandoning Jewish culture for European cultures but rather adding those cultures to the repertoire of East European Jews, at the same time reforming East European Jewish mores and culture. They urged that modern hygienic standards be adopted, secular education be made widely available, and the original Jewish language, Hebrew, displace what they saw as the bastardized "jargon" of Yiddish.[3] A modernized, acculturated Jewry would emerge and prove itself worthy of acceptance by the peoples among whom it dwelled. As one *maskil* put it, "Now that the good graces of the Tsar have appeared among us to lighten our darkness," Jews should "remove their filthy garments which set them off from their neighbors" and reform the rabbinate.[4] Writing in 1866, the poet Judah Leib Gordon called to his fellow Jews:

This land of Eden [Russia] now opens its gates to you
Her sons now call you "brother"!

How long will you dwell among them as a guest,
And why do you now affront them? . . .

Raise your head high, straighten your back,
And gaze with loving eyes upon them,
Open your heart to wisdom and knowledge,
Become an enlightened people and speak their language. . . .

Be a man abroad and a Jew in your tent,
A brother to your countrymen and a servant to your king. . . .[5]

In the Russian Empire, as in most of Europe, complete assimilation entailed adoption of Christianity, which meant a definitive break not only with Judaism but with the Jewish people and with one's own family. Not surprisingly, relatively few were willing to go this far. The alternative of reforming the Jewish appearance, culture, and way of life had a wider appeal. *Haskalah* (enlightenment) was the impetus for the rebirth of Hebrew literature and of attempts to introduce secular education under Jewish auspices. In the empire, however, it did not entail the far-reaching religious changes that it brought about in Western Europe. Reform Judaism remained largely unknown in the Russian Empire.

The pogroms of the 1880s and the reactionary reigns of Tsar Alexander III (1881–94) and Nicholas II (1894–1917) cast a dark shadow on the vision of Jewish acculturation and acceptance into the larger society. Instead of adopting "Europe," many gave up on it. People such as the physician Leon Pinsker were convinced by the pogroms that anti-Semitism was a disease endemic to Europe and could not be eradicated by enlightenment and the rationality on which it was predicated. Instead, drawing from both the traditional Jewish aspiration of *shivat Zion* (return to Zion) and the romantic nationalism then sweeping through Eastern and Central Europe, they argued that Jewish ills could be treated only in an independent Jewish state. Although the leadership of modern political Zionism came initially from Central and Western Europe, the masses who were to turn this seemingly fantastic idea into a movement to be reckoned with were the Jews of the Russian Empire and other areas of Eastern Europe. In the Zionist scheme, the Jews would obtain a territory on which they would create a state. Moreover, many Zionists argued that this state could solve a basic socioeconomic problem by providing land for the Jews to farm, thereby making them physically and economically healthy. The *maskilim* had already pointed to the "lack [of] farmers and plowmen for land they have not had" as a fundamental problem for Jews.[6] Perhaps they were influenced by popular images of "noble savages" and the glories of agricultural labor, as depicted in Tolstoy's *Anna Karenina* and elsewhere in Russian literature. Anyone looking for a solution to the "Jewish problem" would naturally hit on the obvious anomaly of a people deprived of land living in agricultural societies. Socialist Zionists, such as Ber Borochov, A. D. Gordon, and Nachman Syrkin, combined variants of socialism with the Zionist idea in visions of an agricultural, egalitarian society to be created by European migrants to an independent Jewish state in Palestine.

To some Jewish socialists these schemes seemed unrealistic and reactionary. In the late nineteenth century some Jews had joined the *narodnik* (populist) movement, which sought to mobilize the peasantry to overthrow tsarism and establish a just, egalitarian order based on socialist principles. Many, however, became disillusioned by the anti-Jewish actions of peasants. Some of these *narodniks* embraced Marxism as a more promising form of socialism. Marxism identified the proletariat, not the peasantry, as the revolutionary class. It postulated that socialism was inevitable and did not depend on the will of benighted peasants to come to power.[7] By 1897 there were enough Jewish Marxists to found the General League (Bund) of Jewish Workingmen of Russia, Poland, and Lithuania.[8] Though at first committed merely to bringing the message of Marxism to the Yiddish-speaking masses who, they assumed, would learn enough Russian to make a separate Jewish socialist movement unnecessary, the leaders of the Bund found themselves pushed by their nationally conscious constituency to insist on an autonomous Jewish party. Though the Bund helped found the Russian Social Democratic Labor Party (RSDLP) in 1898, it demanded that the party be federal in structure, giving each nationality party considerable autonomy. The Bund's demand that it retain control in matters affecting the Jewish proletariat exclusively was rejected both by the Bolshevik faction of the RSDLP, led by Vladimir Lenin, and by the Mensheviks, led by Iulii Martov, the grandson of a *maskil*, who just a few years earlier had argued the need for an independent Jewish socialist party.[9] Though Lenin and Martov accused the Bund of Jewish nationalism, the Bund rejected Zionism as both unrealistic and reactionary. In the Bund's view, the idea of enticing millions of Jews to migrate to a barren land far from Europe was a chimera. Moreover, by insisting on a Jewish state and attempting to concentrate world Jewry in one territory, Zionists were isolating working-class Jews from the rest of the proletariat and diverting their energies from world revolution to the hopeless task of creating a Jewish state. Furthermore, the attempt to make Hebrew the *Umgangssprache* of the Jews was ridiculous, since it was obvious that Yiddish was the language of the people, especially of the "lower" classes. The solution to the "Jewish question," in the Bund's view, lay in the world socialist revolution. It would abolish all ethnic animosities, disabuse people of the illusions of religion, resolve social and economic conflicts in favor of the downtrodden masses, and lead to the formation of egalitarian, just societies. All peoples would eventually amalgamate, but their ethnocultural needs would be served as long as ethnic groups existed.

Though these ideologies are dazzling in their range and intellectual ingenuity, only a minority of the Russian Empire's Jews became active adherents of one or another.[10] Nearly half the Jews instead "voted with their feet." About two million emigrated, mostly to the United States, Western Europe, and Latin America. Whereas the assimilationists gave up on Jewishness, the *maskilim* on tradition, the Zionists on the diaspora, and the Bund on capitalism and democratic reform, millions gave up on Russia and Europe.

There were three prominent issues in the ideological competition of a century ago that later arose in the Birobidzhan experiment: land and agriculture, language, and autonomy. Those who devised the scheme for an autonomous Jewish region in the Soviet Union were consciously competing with Zionism, as this book makes clear, and tried to provide the most important incentives for settlement that Zionists, Bundists, and emigration advocates had proffered, each in their own ways. They offered economic rehabilitation and social respectability through agricultural work; the preservation and promotion of language, culture—and implicitly—of the Jewish people itself—through compact settlement; and a political structure that would facilitate all of those.

Few would have predicted that Bolsheviks would promote a scheme whose effect would be to consolidate the Jewish population and possibly lead to the establishment of a Jewish territory. After all, before the Bolshevik Revolution both Lenin and Joseph Stalin had vehemently argued that the Jews were not a nation. They lacked the prerequisites for nationhood which Stalin had postulated: a territory, common language, and economy. Lenin condemned discrimination against Jews and prescribed assimilation as the answer to the Jewish problem. He praised the Jews of Western Europe for being in the vanguard of the assimilationists. Once their East European brethren followed suit and amalgamated with other peoples, the Jewish problem would be solved since it stood to reason that if there were no Jews there would be no Jewish problem.

Like the expectation that world revolution would break out in the advanced capitalist countries first and spread immediately to the rest of the world, this schematic, mechanistic conception of the "Jewish problem" and its solution had to be abandoned soon after the revolution. Within a year, the Bolsheviks established Jewish Sections (*Evreiskie sektsii*, or *Evsektsii*) within the Communist Party, though in form, at least, these seemed similar to what the Bund had proposed for the party's predecessor, the RSDLP. A Commissariat for Jewish Affairs (*Evkom*) was set up within the Commissariat of Nationalities, the latter headed by none other than Stalin. Because such a large sector of the Jewish population had only a weak comprehension of Russian, pragmatism won out over principle. Yiddish was used to convey the party's message to the Jewish masses who could not yet be reached in Russian.

Bolshevism had little support among the Jews—there were fewer than a thousand Jews in the Bolshevik ranks before 1917. But once the civil war ended and the Jewish parties were forcibly dissolved, some experienced Jewish socialist and even Zionist activists entered the ranks of the *Evsektsii*, enabling them to launch campaigns to destroy the traditional Jewish way of life and its institutions. The old battle between Yiddish and Hebrew was refought, but this time the weight of state power was thrown behind Yiddish. Hebrew became the only language the Soviets made virtually illegal, as the *Evsektsii* activists persuaded the party that Yiddish was the language of the "toiling masses," whereas Hebrew was the language of the "class enemy," the bourgeoisie, Zionists, and clerics.

Zionism was another target of the *Evsektsii*. Picking up on the critique of Zionism first advanced by the Bund, Lenin, and Stalin, the *Evsektsii* mobilized the Soviet state against Zionist activity and drove Zionists underground, out of the country, to prisons and labor camps, or into political retirement. Finally, the Jewish religion was attacked with a ferocious zeal, which aroused the envy of non-Jewish militant atheists. Judaism was portrayed as superstition, a reactionary ideology which blocked scientific and intellectual progress and which the bourgeoisie had used to divert the attention of the proletariat from its misery.[11]

By the mid-1920s the Communists claimed to have established a monopoly of power "on the Jewish street." Some were content to stop there and let the ineluctable forces of assimilation complete the task they had started by destroying the former Jewish way of life. Others argued that there was still a significant Jewish population that had to be helped toward socialism, either because they were economically dispossessed as former petty traders or self-employed artisans, had vocations made irrelevant by the revolution, or because they were culturally disadvantaged. Still other Jewish Communists saw the preservation of Jewish nationality and culture as a positive goal, though they paid lip service to the ultimate goal of assimilation. The *Evsektsii* had an institutional interest in not declaring victory prematurely because they wanted to justify their continued existence. Their campaigns against Hebrew, Zionism, and Judaism had cleared the way for the construction of a new type of Jewishness and Jewry, and the *Evsektsii* launched several campaigns designed for that purpose.

The first campaign was part of the party and government's drive for *korenizatsiia*, "implanting" Bolshevism among the non-Russians. This would be done by having party and government institutions operate in their languages and educating their children with a Bolshevik content but a national form, as Stalin put it. For Jews this meant the creation of networks of Yiddish schools, newspapers, journals, and theaters. Two academic institutions operating in Yiddish were set up in Kiev and Minsk. Courts, trade unions, and even party cells were encouraged to operate in Yiddish. This was the only time in history that a state invested heavily in Yiddish institutions and the promotion of Yiddish culture. Ironically, the Jews, by and large, rejected this effort. Traditional Jews saw it as an attempt to replace authentic, grassroots Judaism with an ersatz product imposed "from above" by the state, one that would erode Jewish values and traditions, not preserve them. Those uninterested in traditional forms of Jewishness saw no reason to remain loyal to Yiddish culture when the broader horizons of Russian culture beckoned to them. Jews rushed to take advantage of the educational and vocational opportunities the revolution had opened to them. Clearly, Russian was much more useful than Yiddish. As one Jewish porter put it poignantly when the transport workers were discussing the use of Yiddish in union affairs: "For many years I have carried hundreds of pounds on my back, day in and day out. Now I want to learn some Russian and become a *kontorshchik* [office worker]."[12] The Yiddishization campaign failed for the same reasons the language has faded in the United States: as Yiddish speakers moved to the big cities and as younger generations were able to enter higher educational institutions and mainstream occupations, Yiddish seemed outmoded, provincial, and irrelevant, associated with a not very pleasant past. Just as English was seen as the key to Americanization and social mobility by immigrants to the United States, Russian and Russian culture were seen as "higher," more useful, and socially prestigious than the provincial Yiddish by Soviet Jews, many of whom were streaming out of the *shtetlekh* to the larger cities. Therefore, the idea of a territory in which Yiddish would be the dominant language, such as Birobidzhan, had limited appeal to Soviet Jews in the 1920s.

The *Evsektsii* debated whether the small-scale artisans and craftsmen so common among the Jews were self-employed "bourgeois" or whether they were proletarians. Having resolved the issue in favor of working-class status for these *kustar* (artisans), they launched a campaign, "mitn ponim tsum kustar!" (Attention to the artisan!). They promoted cooperatives so that the *kustars* would move from capitalist self-employment to socialist collectivism. This effort was soon eclipsed by the far more ambitious Five-Year Plan (1928), which swept the *kustar*, along with millions of peasants and other workers, into state-owned factories.

The most dramatic effort at constructing a Soviet, secular, socialist Jewry was the attempt to settle Jews on the land. The plan was to settle 100,000 Jews in agricultural colonies within a few years. Earlier, the mystique of agricultural labor had moved Baron Maurice de Hirsch to finance Jewish colonies in the pampas of Argentina; the Am Olam movement settled Jews in colonies in North America; and "territorialist" organizations envisioned the establishment of agriculturally based autonomous Jewish areas in several parts of the world.[13] The "bourgeois" American Jewish Joint Distribution Committee (JDC) and the Jewish Colonization Organization were enthusiastic about the idea of Soviet Jews working the land. In 1928 there were nearly 220,000 Jewish farmers. By the mid-1930s, the JDC had expended $13.8 million on agricultural work and an additional $10.3 million on other assistance. In 1939, when Agro-Joint and ORT (Organization for Rehabilitation and Training) ended their assistance, James Rosenberg, a JDC leader, wrote in an internal report, "Anti-semitism in Russia is a crime. The ghetto dwellers of Russia have been transformed into hardy workers on farms and in factories. For us in the United States there is no Jewish problem in Russia."[14] But collectivization of agriculture and the merger of ethnically distinct collective farms in a process called "internationalization" diminished the attractiveness to Jews of the colonies in Belarus, Ukraine, and the Crimea. The number of Jewish family units on the farms declined from 38,100 in 1926 to 25,000 in 1939.

In the end, the drive to industrialize Russia, the core of Stalin's program, overtook all the schemes the *Evsektsii* and the party had devised for the economic rehabilitation and political socialization of the Jews. The *Evsektsii* were abolished in 1930 and Jewish economic and cultural institutions began to wither. All Soviet nationalities were now mobilized to transform their "common homeland," the Soviet Union, from a backward agricultural state into a modern industrial power. The Birobidzhan project continued to attract support from the state and from some foreign organizations, but as this book makes clear, not very much from Soviet Jews themselves.

As Robert Weinberg makes clear, the Birobidzhan project failed and was probably designed to do so. The agricultural settlements in Ukraine, Belarus, and Crimea, which were within or near the former Pale of Settlement, were more likely to attract and retain Jewish colonists. Clearly, Birobidzhan was designed to buttress Soviet claims to a territory that might be claimed by China or Japan and, perhaps, to ensure the failure of the Jewish colonies in the European republics lest they become the centers of a new Jewish nationalism or even of a "reconstructed" Jewish people. Even if the project was not designed to fail, the fate of Soviet Jewry raises serious questions about the viability of secular Jewishness outside a Jewish state. The secular, socialist Jewishness offered by the *Evsektsii* as a replacement for Judaism and Zionism and traditional ways of life in Birobidzhan and elsewhere did not attract many, just as Yiddishist secularism outside the USSR did not sustain itself much beyond the immigrant generation. The ideologist of Yiddishist secularism, Chaim Zhitlovsky, had confidently asserted that the "Yiddish culture sphere . . . has succeeded in building a 'spiritual-national home,' purely secular, which can embrace all Jews throughout the world. . . . We are beginning to be equal in our national-cultural character with all other cultural peoples in the world."[15] Just as secular Yiddishism failed to prove to be a long-term alternative to traditional forms of Jewish life, so has socialism failed to replace capitalism in most parts of the world. Even the more modest aim of solving the "Jewish problem" in the USSR was not reached by those who directed the Soviet state for over seventy years. Despite claims to having created a "new Soviet man" and to having formed a "society of a new type," where all ethnic tensions were eliminated, in the 1980s *glasnost'* revealed the failures of the system. The fissiparous nationalisms that led to the breakup of not only the former USSR but of Yugoslavia and Czechoslovakia prove dramatically and tragically that the "national question" was not settled by Soviet-style socialism.

Thus, the attempt to create a Jewish Autonomous Region in the Soviet Far East remains largely forgotten in both Soviet and Jewish history. It is so partly because history is written by winners, and Birobidzhan's chief competitors, the Zionists, have emerged triumphant. We need to be reminded, however, that many intelligent and discerning men and women committed themselves strongly to an idea that failed. We should ask why they made that commitment and ponder whatever lessons we think we may derive from this episode. As anyone who has ever conducted a laboratory experiment realizes, we learn as much from failed experiments as we do from the few that are ultimately successful.

NOTES | 1. Surveys of the Jews in the Russian Empire include Salo Baron, *The Russian Jew under Tsars and Soviets* (New York: Macmillan, 1964); S. M. Dubnow, *History of the Jews in Russia and Poland*, 3 vols. (Philadelphia: Jewish Publication Society, 1916–20); and Louis Greenberg, *The Jews in Russia*, 2 vols. (New Haven, Conn.: Yale University Press, 1944). On the government's policy toward the Jews, see John Klier, *Russia Gathers Her Jews* (De Kalb: Northern Illinois University Press, 1986); John Klier, *Imperial Russia's Jewish Question* (Cambridge: Cambridge University Press, 1995); Hans Rogger, *Jewish Policies and Right-Wing Politics in Imperial Russia* (Berkeley and Los Angeles: University of California Press, 1986); and Michael Stanislawski, *Tsar Nicholas I and the Jews* (Philadelphia: Jewish Publication Society, 1983).

2. Recent historical work has questioned the traditional assumption that the pogroms were instigated by the highest authorities, but does confirm that they were

widely tolerated until they threatened to get beyond the control of the civil and police authorities. See, for example, I. Michael Aronson, *Troubled Waters: The Origins of the 1881 Anti-Jewish Pogroms in Russia* (Pittsburgh: University of Pittsburgh Press, 1990), and John Klier and Shlomo Lambroza, eds., *Pogroms: Anti-Jewish Violence in Modern Russian History* (Cambridge: Cambridge University Press, 1992).

3. On the enlightenment (*haskalah*) in the Russian Empire, see Eli Lederhandler, *The Road to Modern Jewish Politics* (New York: Oxford University Press, 1989); Jacob Raisin, *The Haskalah Movement in Russia* (Philadelphia: Jewish Publication Society, 1914); and Michael Stanislawski, *For Whom Do I Toil* (New York: Oxford University Press, 1988).

4. S. J. Fuenn, "The Need for Enlightenment (1840)," in *The Jew in the Modern World*, ed. Paul Mendes-Flohr and Jehuda Reinharz, 2d ed. (New York: Oxford University Press, 1985), 381, 382.

5. Judah Leib Gordon, "Awake My People! (1866)," in Mendes-Flohr and Reinharz, *The Jew in the Modern World*, 384. Perhaps a better rendering of the last line (*heye ben adam betsaytecha, viyehudi beoholekha*) might be, "Be a regular person on the street, and a Jew at home."

6. Fuenn, "The Need for Enlightenment," 381.

7. On Jews in the Populist movement and that movement's position on the "Jewish question," see Yitzhak Maor, *She'elat haYehudim batnuah haliberalit vehamehapchanit berusiya* (The Jewish Question in the Liberal and Revolutionary Movement in Russia) (Jerusalem: Mosad Bialik, 1964); Viktor Chernov, *Yidishe tuer in der partai sotsialistn revolutsionern* (Jewish Activists in the Socialist-Revolutionary Party) (New York: Workmen's Circle, 1948); and Erich Haberer, *Jews and Revolution in Nineteenth-Century Russia* (Cambridge: Cambridge University Press, 1995).

8. On the emergence of a Jewish labor movement, see Ezra Mendelsohn, *Class Struggle in the Pale* (Cambridge: Cambridge University Press, 1970), and Moshe Mishkinsky, *Reshit tnuat hapoalim hayehudit berusiya* (The Origins of the Jewish Labor Movement in Russia) (Tel Aviv: Hakibbutz Hameuchad and Tel Aviv University, 1981).

9. See Henry Jack Tobias, *The Jewish Bund in Russia* (Stanford, Calif.: Stanford University Press, 1972).

10. An extensive treatment of these ideologies and movements is Jonathan Frankel, *Prophecy and Politics* (Cambridge: Cambridge University Press, 1981).

11. For details, see Zvi Gitelman, *Jewish Nationality and Soviet Politics* (Princeton, N.J.: Princeton University Press, 1972) chap. 5.

12. *Der emes* (The Truth; Moscow), April 6, 1924.

13. On pre-Soviet Jewish agricultural colonization in the Russian Empire, see Zvi Livneh-Liberman et al., *Khaklaim yehudim bearvot rusiya* (Jewish Agriculturalists on the Russian Steppes) (Tel Aviv: Sifriat Poalim, 1965), and Zvi Livneh (Liberman), *Ikarim yehudim berusiya* (Jewish Farmers in Russia) (Tel Aviv: Alef, 1967). On Zionist agricultural colonies, see Yehuda Erez, *Khalutzim hayinu berusiya* (We Were Pioneers in Russia) (Tel Aviv: Am Oved, 1976).

14. Quoted in Zvi Gitelman, "Gorbachev's Reforms and the Future of Soviet Jewry," *Soviet Jewish Affairs* 18, no. 2 (1988): 4. Rosenberg also wrote *On the Steppes*

(New York: Knopf, 1927), an enthusiastic account of Jewish agricultural colonization. In a letter to his grandnephew, Peter Solomon, Rosenberg described the Crimean settlement program as "the greatest effort of my life. We settled over 300,000 Jews in the Crimea and made them—or rather they made themselves—into fine successful farmers. Then came World War Two. The Crimea which we thought was a safe place was overrun by Hitler hordes. Stalin completed the gruesome job of mass murder. So this great effort . . . ended in bitter nothingness. Never since 1938 have I heard a single word from any of those Jews" (dated August 18, 1959, courtesy of Professor Peter Solomon, University of Toronto). Rosenberg also sponsored a trip to the colonies by Evelyn Morrissey, who then published her impressions as *Jewish Workers and Farmers in the Crimea and Ukraine* (New York: privately printed, 1937).

15. Quoted in "What is Secular Jewish Culture?" in *The Way We Think*, ed. Joseph Leftwich (New York: Thomas Yoseloff, 1969), 1:93.

View of the J.A.R. countryside, mid-1930s.

THE BIROBIDZHAN PROJECT

In May 1934 the Soviet government established the Jewish Autonomous Region (J.A.R.) in a remote, sparsely populated region of the Soviet Far East. Located along the Sino-Soviet border some five thousand miles east of Moscow, the J.A.R.—popularly known as Birobidzhan, the region's capital city—was designated the national homeland of Soviet Jewry. The Birobidzhan project met with great fanfare both in the Soviet Union and abroad and marked the culmination of an effort begun in the 1920s. The creation of the J.A.R. was part of the Communist Party's effort to set up a territorial enclave where a secular Jewish culture rooted in Yiddish and socialist principles could serve as an alternative to Palestine and resolve a variety of perceived problems besetting Soviet Jewry. The notion of a Jewish homeland appealed to many Soviet Jews, and the Birobidzhan project was intended to undercut the Zionist focus on Palestine.

The J.A.R. still exists today; there one can still buy a Yiddish newspaper, study Yiddish at the local teachers' college, and listen to a weekly Yiddish radio program. However, Jews always have been a small minority of the inhabitants of the J.A.R. and by no means has the region ever embodied the national or cultural aspirations of Soviet Jews. In 1939, for example, on the eve of World War II, Jews constituted just under 20 percent of the region's population; by 1989 the proportion of Jews had dropped precipitously to under 5 percent. The Jews of Birobidzhan have lived the fiction that they inhabited the national homeland of Soviet Jewry. But with the dissolution of the Soviet Union, they now find themselves confronted with the challenge of transforming this fiction into a reality. Like Jews all over the former Soviet Union, they are wrestling with the problem of Jewish identity on both an individual and a communal level and are engaged in a renaissance of Jewish cultural and religious life, despite the fact that decades of Soviet power and, in the past twenty years, emigration have vitiated Jewish life.

Besides examining the reasons behind the Soviet leadership's decision to establish the J.A.R., this book offers a glimpse into the lives of those Jews who chose to settle in Birobidzhan. What was (and is) specifically Jewish about the

J.A.R., and how did the Soviet leadership set about to transplant Russian Jewish culture and society to the region? How was Jewish life promoted in a stridently secular and militantly antireligious setting, and how did the Soviet government promote the Birobidzhan project to both the Soviet public and the international community? What elements of Jewish culture survived under Soviet power, and how have they provided the foundation for the current Jewish cultural and religious activism in the J.A.R.?

The story of the Soviet Zion provides an unusual point of entry for examining the Kremlin's shifting policies toward Jews and the fate of Soviet Jewry under Communist rule. This perspective also permits us to assess the response of world Jewry to the novel experiment undertaken in the J.A.R. Given the persistence of the "Jewish question" in Russia for the last two hundred years, the study of the J.A.R. has several implications. First, it sheds light on a host of important historical and contemporary issues regarding Jewish identity, community, and culture. Second, the history of Birobidzhan illuminates the larger issue of Soviet policies toward ethnic and national minorities and illustrates how such policies have left a lasting legacy during the challenging transition from communism to democracy in the former Soviet Union.

The collapse of the tsarist regime in the wake of World War I and the consolidation of Bolshevik rule by 1921 ushered in an age of unprecedented freedom for Russia's Jews. The nearly two and a half million Jews then living under Soviet power enjoyed the same civil and political liberties as other citizens. Despite the militant atheism of the Communist Party, many Jews welcomed

"What is a nation?...A nation is a historically constituted, stable community of people, formed on the basis on a common language, territory, economic life, and psychological makeup manifested in a common culture....Among the Jews there is no large and stable stratum connected with the land, which would naturally rivet the nation together." Joseph Stalin, "Marxism and the Nationality Question" (1913).

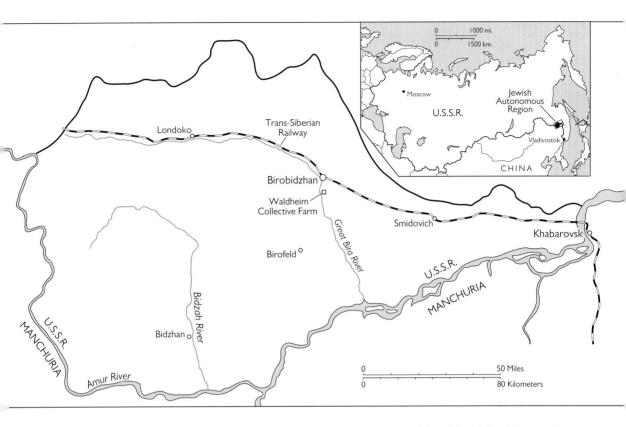

Map of the J.A.R., with inset of the Soviet Union.

Bolshevik rule because the new masters in the Kremlin promised an end to social and economic inequality, offered new employment opportunities, and took a strong public stance against anti-Semitism. The Bolsheviks professed a commitment to the rights of national and ethnoreligious minorities, and Soviet nationality policy in the 1920s—the era of the New Economic Policy—was relatively open: all national and ethnic cultures were tolerated, though some of their specific features, such as religion, were combatted. Cultural diversity was allowed if it was "national in form and socialist in content."[1]

However, the reality of ruling a multinational empire with well over one hundred national and ethnoreligious groups left the fledgling Soviet leadership with no choice but to acknowledge the diversity of the Soviet Union's populace. Vladimir Lenin and Joseph Stalin, the Bolsheviks' leading theorists on nationality policy, believed that socialism would doom to extinction all religious

Like most Jews living in tsarist Russia, this peddler eked out a meager existence and was required to reside within the borders of the Pale of Settlement, which consisted of the empire's western and southwestern provinces.

and nationalist sentiments and loyalties. In the long run, all cultures would fuse with each other to form a common socialist Soviet culture. Until that time, each national and ethnoreligious minority would be permitted to maintain its cultural and linguistic traditions and continue to reside in its territory of traditional settlement. According to Lenin and Stalin, the Jewish question would ultimately be solved by facilitating the integration of Jews into Soviet society. With the disappearance of religion under socialism, the secularization of Soviet Jewish society would proceed smoothly and weaken obstacles to Jewish acculturation and integration.

The Kremlin was also concerned about the Jews' grinding poverty, unrelenting unemployment, and overpopulation, as well as the resurgent popular anti-Semitism and vicious pogroms in the years after the Soviet seizure of power. The overwhelming majority of Soviet Jews lived in small towns and cities, and made livings from petty commerce, retail sales, small-scale handicraft production, and unskilled labor. They were particularly hard hit by the collapse of the economy due to the combined impact of world war, revolution, civil war, and pogroms between 1914 and 1921.

The number of Jews out of work reached startling proportions in the early 1920s. In the area around the city of Gomel in Belarus, Jews constituted some

Map of the Pale of Settlement.

70 percent of the unemployed. Moreover, despite the fact that private trade was tolerated in the 1920s in an attempt to revive the wrecked economy and restore social peace, the government continued its policy of nationalizing private property. By the early 1920s, then, many Soviet Jews occupying traditional trades and crafts were suffering from the impact of political unrest, civil strife, and economic breakdown.

Backed by the Jewish Sections, the arm of the Communist Party that conducted propaganda among Jews, the government was concerned about the dire economic straits of the Jewish masses and encouraged their settlement on the land. As defined by Communist officials, one aspect of the Jewish question was the ideologically suspect nature of Jewish economic life. Thus, the government hoped to resolve the Jewish question in the 1920s by refashioning the occupational profile of the Jews and transforming them into farmers.

Tsarist attitudes and policies helped to shape certain features of the Communists' approach to the Jews. The Bolshevik conviction to alter the socioeconomic structure of Jewish society had its roots in the late eighteenth century, when, as a result of the partitions of Poland, the Russian Empire absorbed a substantial Jewish population. Tsarist policy toward the Jews was contradictory, since it combined efforts to integrate Jews into Russian society with attempts to keep them segregated from the mainstream. These policies, enacted through such measures as enforced Jewish residence within the Pale of Settlement and enrollment in secular schools, worked at cross purposes and characterized tsarist treatment of the Jews until the collapse of the Romanov dynasty in 1917.

One aspect of the Jewish question, as defined by tsarist officials, was the perceived unproductive nature of Jewish economic life. Because the Jews were heavily involved in leaseholding, commerce, moneylending, and the sale of vodka, tsarist officials regarded them as parasites who exploited the defenseless peasantry. Thus, some tsars such as Alexander I tried to "normalize" the socioeconomic profile of Russian Jewry by encouraging Jews to till the land or become small-scale manufacturers. The solution to the Jewish question, therefore, depended on transforming the Jews from a harmful and retrograde community to one incapable of causing social and economic damage. Such thinking had also characterized the Jewish policies pursued by some other European states in the eighteenth and nineteenth centuries.

This experiment in social engineering never achieved its desired ends, in part because Russian Jews resisted changing livelihoods, preferring instead work with which they had experience and familiarity. In addition, the government's commitment to agricultural resettlement was halfhearted and never received serious financial and other material support. More important, other policies designed to isolate the Jews countered the policy of land resettlement and dominated the autocracy's Jewish policy at the end of the imperial era. Indeed, Jews were prohibited from settling on the land in the wake of the assassination of Tsar Alexander II in 1881. Nevertheless, on the eve of World War I slightly more than fifty thousand Jews (or 3 percent of the total Jewish population in the Russian Empire), including the family of Leon Trotsky, tilled land as agricultural settlers. The overwhelming number of Jews remained engaged in commerce, manufacturing, and the service sector by the end of the nineteenth century.

Workers dig a well in a Jewish agricultural colony in Crimea, 1928.

The effort to render Jews harmless by making them more like the peasantry and thereby promoting their integration into Russian society also shaped government policy toward Soviet Jewry during the 1920s. Just as tsarist bureaucrats hoped to refashion the occupational profile of Russian Jewry, Soviet policy makers also hoped that the settlement of Jews on the land would reduce the number of Jews involved in commerce, retail sales, and handicraft production. This "normalization" or "productivization" of Jewry—also a Zionist objective —would presumably weaken popular anti-Semitism as well as promote the integration of Jews into an emerging socialist economy and society. Given the devastated condition of Soviet industry in the 1920s, government officials focused on agricultural resettlement as a strategy. Despite the long-term objective of presiding over an industrialized society, the Kremlin in the 1920s did not pursue a concerted policy of industrialization that could absorb significant numbers of economically marginal Jews. The publication of two issues of the journal *Evreiskii krest' ianin* (The Jewish Peasant) in 1925 and 1926 underscores this official interest in Jewish land resettlement.

This Soviet propaganda poster shows that the *kheder*, the one-room Jewish primary school, produces a slavish attitude and leads to undesirable consequences such as religious observance and practice, enmity among peoples, and petty commerce. In contrast, the Soviet school prepares healthy people, capable of building a socialist society in which agricultural labor, factory work, and amity among peoples are primary objectives. The Yiddish reads: "The old school produced slaves; the Soviet school prepares healthy, skilled workers who are builders of the socialist order. The *kheder* [left] leads to the shop, synagogue, and hatred between peoples. The Soviet school [right] leads to the factory, land, and unity between peoples." Color lithograph, 1920s. 42 ⅛ × 23 ⅜ in.

In the mid-1920s the government oversaw the formation of two organizations: OZET (Society for the Settlement of Jewish Toilers on the Land) and KOMZET (Committee for the Settlement of Jewish Toilers on the Land). OZET, ostensibly a public organization devoted to publicizing the settlement of Soviet Jewry on the land, was controlled by KOMZET members, primarily government employees and Communist officials, who oversaw the organization of Jewish land settlement in Ukraine, Belarus, and the Crimea. At first, these organizations devoted their efforts to encouraging Jewish settlement in these areas but turned their attention to the J.A.R. after 1928. The organized movement of shtetl Jews to the land supplemented the spontaneous drift of Jews into agriculture that had occurred during World War I, the Bolshevik Revolution, and the ensuing civil war. By 1930 some 47,000 Jewish families, or approximately 231,000 persons, were engaged in agricultural activities throughout the Soviet Union.

TAMING THE TAIGA | Mystery shrouds the 1928 decision to designate the Biro-Bidzhanskii District as the official territory for Jewish land resettlement. The region, approximately the size of Belgium, had been annexed by Russia in 1858 and derived its name from two tributaries of the Amur River, the Bira and the Bidzhan, that flowed through the territory. Summers in the area are hot and rainy; winters are dry and cold. Rich in natural resources, particularly in the north, where mountains and thick forests punctuate the landscape, the Biro-Bidzhanskii District then had large tracts of swampland and marshes. Along with several hundred indigenous Siberian peoples who subsisted on hunting and gathering, the twenty-seven thousand or so inhabitants residing there on the eve of Jewish settlement were primarily Great Russians, Cossacks, Koreans, and Ukrainians who had gone to the region in the late nineteenth and early twentieth centuries. Placement was concentrated in the south, along the Amur River, and in the north, around the Trans-Siberian Railway.

Attracting Jews to the Soviet Far East was an integral part of a plan to lure Soviet Jewry to the land as early as the beginning of 1924. Though a contingent of leading Jewish activists in KOMZET and the Jewish Sections of the Communist Party vociferously opposed the Birobidzhan experiment because they thought the region too far from the pocket of Jewish population to be viable, they were overridden by Stalin and other proponents of the project. The government intended to vitiate the movement of Jews to the land in Ukraine, Belarus, and the Crimea to appease the native populace, which was resisting plans to settle more Jews in these regions. In addition, officials in the Commissariats of Defense and Agriculture also had an eye toward establishing a strong presence in the Soviet Far East. The area possessed untapped economic resources and had geostrategic significance given fears of possible Chinese and Japanese expansionism in the 1920s.

Furthermore, many in the Kremlin were interested in creating a Jewish national territory within the borders of the Soviet Union. Soviet Jewry, like several other extraterritorial minorities such as the Volga Germans, occupied an anomalous position because they lacked a national territory. Soviet policy in the 1920s aimed at normalizing the status of nonterritorial minorities by establishing official enclaves for them. However, what made granting Soviet Jews their own territory a special case was that the place selected for them was not one in which they had roots. The obvious comparison with Palestine was not ignored by advocates of Birobidzhan, and many interested observers, such as I. Sudarskii in his book *Birobidzhan and Palestine* (Yiddish version in 1929, Russian in 1930), argued that Birobidzhan was more suitable for Jewish settlement than Palestine.

Proponents of the Birobidzhan project believed that the establishment of a territorial homeland for Soviet Jews would facilitate the development of a secular, Yiddishist culture rooted in socialist principles, while at the same time ensuring the national and cultural consolidation of Soviet Jewry. The president of the Soviet Union, Mikhail Kalinin, had adopted the creation of Jewish territory as a pet project in order to preserve Jewish culture. In 1926 Kalinin declared:

[I]t is completely natural that the Jewish population . . . strives to find its place in the Soviet Union. . . . The Jewish people faces the great task of preserving its own nationality, and to this end a large part of the Jewish population must be transformed into an economically stable, agriculturally compact group which should number at least hundreds of thousands. Only under such conditions can the Jewish masses hope for the future existence of their nationality.[2]

The settlement of Jews in the J.A.R. would transform the shtetl Jew from petit-bourgeois shopkeepers and unskilled laborers into productive Soviet citizens contributing to the building of socialism.

The government began encouraging Jews to move to the J.A.R. soon after the publication of a March 1928 decree reserving the Biro-Bidzhanskii District for the settlement of Jews who would work the land. The decree banned agricul-

Cover of Yiddish edition of I. Sudarskii, *Birobidzhan and Palestine* (1929).

Mikhail Kalinin, president of the USSR, shown addressing a 1926 conference of the OZET, an ostensibly nongovernmental organization devoted to publicizing the agricultural settlement of Soviet Jews.

tural settlement by non-Jews and stated that if Jewish settlement were successful, "a Jewish national, administrative-territorial entity" might be set up. This dream was realized in 1934, when the district was designated as the Jewish Autonomous Region, with Birobidzhan as its capital city, thereby establishing it as the national territory of Soviet Jewry. As stated above, the guiding principle behind Jewish land resettlement in the J.A.R. was to make Soviet Jews more productive by attracting unskilled, poverty-stricken Jews to agricultural work in the region. No less an authority than Semen Dimanshtein, chairman of OZET and a prominent party official in charge of Jewish affairs, wrote that the organized settlement of the J.A.R. would "strengthen the tempo of the productivization of the Jewish poor."[3] Another supporter of attracting Jews to agricultural labor noted that it would lead to the "physical rebirth and renewal" of Soviet Jewry. As one of the first Jews to move to the region stated, "I thank you, comrades, for sending me here. Here I am getting settled and will stop living life like a 'Jew,' that is, as a *luftmentsh*" (literally, a person who lives on air, that is, with no visible means of support, a common way to refer to poor Jews). As one Jewish migrant to a rice plantation in the southern part of the J.A.R. stressed soon after his arrival in 1928, perhaps speaking for others who saw themselves as pioneers, "We came here to become peasants!"[4]

Incentives were made strong to attract impoverished Jews to the J.A.R. The government provided migrants and members of their families with either free or significantly discounted travel and food subsidies. It also extended

Document authorizing travel to and settlement in the J.A.R., 1939. The document states that the settler "enjoys all rights and privileges provided by law." 4 × 6 in.

credit, tax exemptions, and other material benefits to those who engaged in agriculture. Persons interested in taking advantage of incentives were required to register with their local KOMZET office, which then arranged resettlement through the Commissariat of Agriculture. In accord with the state's desire to productivize Soviet Jewry, Jews who had been categorized as "nonlaborers" would regain their electoral rights in the J.A.R. if they engaged in agricultural and other forms of work considered productive and socially useful by the government.

But the authorities did little to prepare the newcomers, most of whom had no agricultural experience, for the hardships in an unknown and forbidding region. Nor did the government provide the settlers with decent housing, food, medical care, and working conditions. The harsh realities of daily life in the J.A.R. during the initial years of settlement contrasted starkly with the promises and public pronouncements of the government. In many instances, Jewish pioneers found they were given land unsuitable for cultivation because it had not been drained and surveyed. In other cases, the fledgling collective and state farms, chronically mismanaged and poorly organized, often lacked basic necessities such as potable water, barns, livestock, tools, and equipment.

Viktor Fink, a Soviet journalist who accompanied an American fund-raising organization traveling to the J.A.R. in 1929, wrote a scathing account of the horrendous conditions he encountered. In Tikhonkaia, the railway station at which

Jews interested in moving to the J.A.R. apply at a KOMZET office in Minsk, late 1920s.

the vast majority of newly arrived migrants disembarked and which grew rapidly into the city of Birobidzhan in a few short years, settlers lived in makeshift barracks which "would put prisons to shame." Even though the barracks were designed as temporary lodging before the migrants were sent to work the land, many Jews found themselves in Tikhonkaia for two or three months because their place of destination was not ready or there was no way to traverse the swamps and marshes that dotted the region. Appalled by the substandard living and working conditions, others returned to Tikhonkaia after venturing into the countryside to their designated place of settlement. In one instance, settlers arrived at a tract of land some thirty miles from Tikhonkaia, only to learn that no one had bothered to survey the land, which had no potable water. Many families quickly went through their meager food allocations and loans and were reduced to a state of penury. Begging proliferated and some women turned to prostitution in order to subsist. Fink concluded that the cause of these problems was the absence of any planning for how to absorb the sudden influx of newcomers. In his words, "the colonization of Birobidzhan was begun and executed without preparation, planning and study.

Jewish migrants after their arrival at the train station in Tikhonkaia a small village along the Trans-Siberian Railway. Chief point of disembarkation for people moving to the J.A.R., Tikhonkaia grew rapidly after 1928, was renamed Birobidzhan several years later, and became the capital of the J.A.R.

All the misfortunes are due to the hasty manner" in which the Birobidzhan project was implemented.[5]

Other accounts testify to the trials and tribulations of many of the first pioneers to the region: wagons became mired in impassable, muddy roads, and the settlers had to haggle with officials over their land allotments; all contended with particularly fierce mosquitoes until the land was drained and reclaimed; everyone had to make due with livestock stricken with a variety of diseases. In some instances, the migrants had to sleep out-of-doors until tents arrived and barracks were erected. Primitive medical facilities were frequently located miles away from the new settlements. And to make matters worse, massive floods covered the J.A.R. in 1928 and 1932, destroying crops and forcing some collective and state farms to start anew.

Local officials were ill-prepared to handle the arrival of hundreds of Jewish migrants. Understaffed and plagued by inadequate supplies, equipment, and poor planning, the government organs in charge of settling Jewish pioneers were not up to the task and bore the brunt of complaints lodged by many of the settlers. Agricultural resettlement also foundered because most of the Jew-

Jewish family outside its home in the late 1920s or early 1930s. The underground house is known as a *zemlianka,* a mud hut with sod and thatch built over a hole in the ground.

ВАЛДГЕМ וואלדהיים

Founded in 1928 under the direction of L. Gefen, Waldheim was the first Jewish collective farm established in the J.A.R. Waldheim was located near Tikhonkaia and had its start when thirty-two settlers erected tents and began to clear the land.

In 1929 an American expedition under the leadership of Franklin
Harris, an agronomist and president of Brigham Young University,
visited the J.A.R. They returned to the United States and
publicized the viability of the J.A.R. for agricultural settlement and
develop-ment. These images are from *A Scientific Expedition to Birobidzhan,* a six-minute reel shot by the expedition during its travels.

ish migrants chose not to start new lives engaged in agriculture. The overwhelming majority of Jews who came to the J.A.R. in its early years had little
or no firsthand knowledge of farming, and many were unprepared psycho-
logically and physically for the rigorous demands of pioneer life. Indeed, in
1928, the first year of settlement, no Jewish settlers had agricultural experience
or had any idea how to clear and drain the land, let alone cultivate it. According to a 1932 KOMZET report on the J.A.R., of the 6,200 Jews who had gone
to the region during the first six months of that year, most had lived in large
towns and cities in Belarus and Ukraine and had worked as blacksmiths, car-
penters, tinsmiths, woodworkers, and tailors.

This 1936 decree granting the residents of the Culture and Labor Collective Farm "eternal use of the land" was enhanced with use of gold lettering (on the cover) and watercolor (on the map). The government gave similar decrees to other collective farms throughout the Soviet Union. Although the members of the collective possessed the right to cultivate the land, the state retained ownership of it. In practice, the state controlled all aspects of the operations of the collective farm. This decree, in Yiddish and Russian, indicated the precise size and location of the collective farm. 14 × 21 in. (closed).

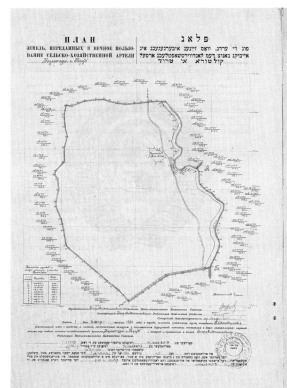

This certificate of merit was awarded to Alec Belzer in 1932 for his outstanding contribution as "a builder of socialism." The certificate reads at the top: "We Will Fulfill the Five-Year Plan in Four Years at an Urgent Pace." Offset color lithograph, 1932. 12 × 8 ½ in.

Bread store in Birobidzhan, 1937. The slogan behind the sales clerks states, "Workers of the Soviet State and Cooperative Retail Trade Struggle to Provide Polite and Improved Service to the Soviet Customer in the town and countryside."

Therefore, it is no surprise that the population of the J.A.R. during its early years remained highly mobile, continually searching for viable niches outside agriculture. Furthermore, the dismal state of affairs throughout the J.A.R. contributed to a high drop-out rate for Jewish settlers. During the first decade of its existence approximately 35,000–40,000 Jews moved to the region, though most chose not to remain there. The yearly drop-out rate among Jewish settlers reached 50 percent and even higher during the first several years of settlement as Jews either left the countryside for life in one of the larger cities of the Soviet Far East, such as Khabarovsk or Vladivostok, or returned to their native homes. Those Jews who did choose to remain were more likely to gravitate to the capital city of Birobidzhan and to nonagricultural employment with which they had prior experience—work in the retail and service sectors, for example, or in government offices. More important, Jews had no historical roots in the region and were wary of starting life anew in an unknown and forbidding part of the Soviet Union. They were understandably reluctant to pick up and move several thousand miles to endure an arduous existence as agricultural settlers. It is hard to see how the designation of a remote territory, a good portion of which was unsuitable for agriculture—given the abundance of swamps, marshes, and mountains—could have served as a magnet for the impoverished.

That Jews were attracted to nonagricultural employment should also be understood in the context of the priorities of the planned economy emphasizing industrial development and the modernization of agriculture through the creation of state and collective farms. Begun in earnest soon after the settlement of Birobidzhan was initiated, the concerted industrialization drive of the Soviet Union diluted the government's effort to resolve the "Jewish question" through agrarianization. By the early 1930s the specifically agricultural aim of Jewish resettlement in the J.A.R. had been watered down by the government's decision to step up the diverse and broadly based economic development of the region, a policy in accordance with a 1931 decree to transform the territory into an autonomous administrative entity for Soviet Jews by late 1933. Manufacturing, construction, and the extraction and processing of the region's natural resources (timber, fish, limestone, iron ore, tin, coal, copper, graphite, and even gold) were never entirely ignored by government planners. The promotion of well-rounded economic growth was necessary to develop the region's infrastructure and satisfy the diverse needs of the populace; it was essential that some of the settlers engage in manufacturing, construction, and sales and clerical work to make a living as well as to provide support services to those working in agriculture. In addition, many Jews who moved to the land may have been disappointed that they were treated by the state as proletarians or farm

Front page of *Bolshevik Sowing* (May 1932). The lead article cautions against overconfidence in a successful sowing campaign. The Russian headline exhorts workers to devote "all energy and will to the completion of planting 6,000 hectares of soybeans ahead of schedule." Note the Yiddish masthead and headline, which suggests that the editors were targeting both Jewish and non-Jewish audiences, particularly those involved in agriculture. The headline in Yiddish proclaims, "Watch the machines, prevent accidents, work hard and with devotion as shock workers," that is, as those who overfulfill production quotas.

laborers employed on state farms. What they wanted was the opportunity to become individual farmers tilling their own land. Thus, one of the goals of settling the J.A.R. was never reached; by 1939 only 25 percent (4,404 of 17,695) of the total Jewish population in the territory lived in the countryside, and not all of these Jews engaged in agricultural pursuits. The plan to resettle large numbers of Jews on the land was stillborn.

Despite the failure of Jewish agricultural settlement, Soviet citizens—both Jewish and gentile—nevertheless chose to uproot themselves and settle the J.A.R. For example, in the 1970s Yakov Blekhman, a resident of the J.A.R. since the mid-1930s, recounted that the Odessa Young Communist League sent him to the Soviet Far East in 1934 as a construction worker. He eventually ended up in Birobidzhan after listening to a recruiter for Jewish settlers from the J.A.R.[6] The Kremlin spearheaded a campaign designed not only to publicize the Birobidzhan experiment but also to raise funds and to encourage migration to the region. For example, a feature-length film entitled *Seekers of Happiness* was released in 1936. Partially filmed in the J.A.R., the film starred several prominent Yiddish actors, including Benjamin Zuskin. It told the story of a Jewish family who moved to the J.A.R. from abroad to escape the travails of the Great Depression and to find happiness and fulfillment building the "Soviet Zion." In addition, OZET promoted public awareness of the J.A.R. and raised funds for the region by holding a series of lotteries. OZET commissioned the well-known Jewish graphic artist Mikhail Dlugach (1893–1988) to design a series of posters that publicized the lotteries in an effort to build socialism in the J.A.R. Born in Odessa, Dlugach rose to prominence in Moscow, where he was one of the few Jewish graphic artists to remain at the top of the art world

Front page of *Forest Worker in the Taiga of Birobidzhan* (January 1932). The lead article discusses the output of various work brigades involved in felling trees. The article criticizes those brigades not meeting their production quotas.

The well-known Yiddish actor Benjamin Zuskin as Pinya, the lead character in the 1936 feature-length film *Seekers of Happiness*.

This poster depicts a deserted shtetl (center right), where a family is loading a horse and wagon for a journey to the J.A.R. and a new life as agricultural workers. The slogan surrounding the family states, "Every OZET lottery ticket bought will increase the number of Jewish agricultural laborers." The slogan in the top right corner reads, "We will finish with the old more quickly if we participate in the OZET lottery." The slogan at the bottom states, "To the green new shoots of the laboring fields." Color lithograph poster for second lottery, 1929. 28 ⅛ × 43 ⅛ in.

This poster applauds the 1931 decision of the Central Executive Committee of the USSR to establish by late 1933 a Jewish Autonomous Region within the borders of Birobidzhan. The text states that Birobidzhan is "one of the components of Leninist nationality policy." Color lithograph poster, 1933. 33 ⅛ × 23 ¼ in.

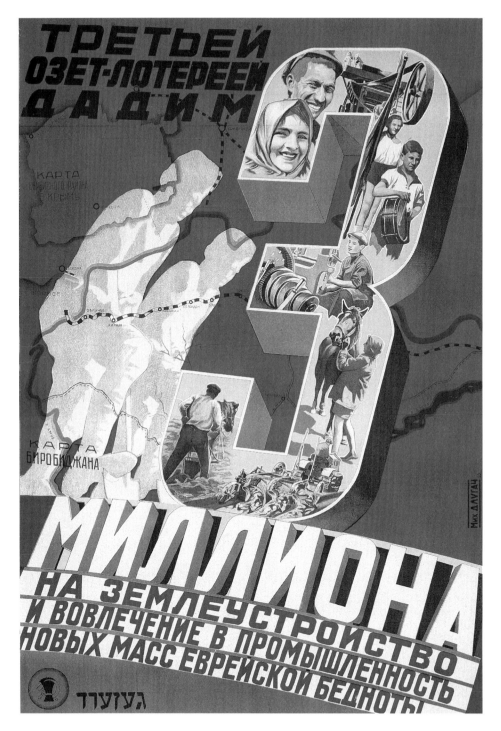

This poster shows Jews plowing the land and a map of the J.A.R.
The text reads, "Let us give millions to settle poor Jews on the
land and to attract them to industry." Color lithograph poster for
third lottery, 1930. 41 ⅛ × 27 ⅞ in.

The text proclaims, "Build a socialist Birobidzhan" and "Strengthen the great achievements of Leninist nationality policy." Note the prominent display of tractors and the soldier standing guard, presumably a reference to the Kremlin's concern with the invasion of Manchuria (which borders the J.A.R.) by the Japanese army in mid-1931. Color lithograph poster for fourth lottery, 1931. 41 ⅛ × 26 ¼ in.

This poster appeals to the public "to build a socialist Birobidzhan, the future Jewish Autonomous Region" by buying a lottery ticket for fifty kopecks. Color lithograph poster for fourth lottery, 1931. 27 × 20 in.

The "Birobidzhanets."

during the 1930s. The organization also dubbed an airplane the "Birobidzhanets" and had it traverse Belarus and Ukraine as part of a publicity stunt to raise funds. During a two-week trip in 1933, the "Birobidzhanets" covered some five thousand kilometers and distributed pamphlets and other propaganda.

Life in the J.A.R. gradually improved from the time the first settlers arrived in 1928, though serious problems such as insufficient housing and food and inadequate medical and sanitary facilities continued to plague both rural and urban residents. The ongoing influx of people taxed the ability of local officials to meet the needs of the region's burgeoning population. In 1935 a medical doctor touring the Soviet Far East visited the J.A.R. and decried the "disgraceful unsanitary" conditions of Birobidzhan, where "there are two or three garbage pits in every courtyard" and the streets and squares are never cleaned.[7] A 1937 report stated that the city of Birobidzhan, with ten thousand residents by 1936, still lacked a sewage system and public lighting.

Despite these shortcomings, the J.A.R. grew steadily throughout the 1930s. It became an important source of cement, tin, bricks, paper products, and clothing. The capital city of Birobidzhan grew into a city of approximately thirty thousand inhabitants by the eve of World War II. Thus, the growth of

Ticket for second OZET lottery, 1929. 4 ⅛ × 5 ¾ in.

Preparation of lumber used for
constructing barracks and other
buildings in Tikhonkaia.

Construction of Lenin Square,
the center of Birobidzhan.

Laying the first stones of paved
road in front of the Birobidzhan
train station in 1936.

View of the completed road in front of the Birobidzhan train station several months after work had begun. The wooden barracks, which were to serve as temporary lodging for newcomers, had become perm-anent residences for many inhab-itants of Birobidzhan.

View of Birobidzhan's major thoroughfare in 1938. It was renamed Sholom Aleichem Street in 1946 on the thirtieth anniversary of the great Yiddish writer's death.

the region paralleled the swift development of the Soviet Far East in the 1930s.

The issue of populating the Soviet Far East had been the subject of intense discussion during the 1920s, and the government had decided to promote the development of the region through planned resettlement, primarily on the land. Appeals went out throughout the Soviet Union, claiming that the Soviet Far East was a land of opportunity for those willing to take the risk. But it was not until the implementation of the command economy with its Five-Year Plans that the Soviet Far East witnessed a swift and steady rise in its population.

Not unexpectedly, large numbers of non-Jews found their way to the J.A.R. via channels not under the supervision of KOMZET, especially since local

This red silk banner was a gift from the workers of Kharkiv (Ukraine) to the J.A.R. in 1935 on the first anniversary of its existence as an autonomous region. The quotation is from Stalin and states in both Yiddish and Ukrainian: "Be true to the cause of proletarian internationalism, the cause of fraternal unity, and the proletarians of all countries." Silk-embroidered image on silk velvet (Ukrainian side) and cotton and silk twill (Yiddish side) with appliqué and metal-wrapped thread fringe, 1935. 52 × 61 ½ in.

officials, ever aware of the acute labor shortage, were eager to populate the region with able-bodied persons regardless of ethnic, national, or religious background. Indeed, the Second Five-Year Plan (1933–37) set an overly ambitious population target of 300,000 for the J.A.R. But only half of these were to be Jews. The building of socialism required labor, and given the flux and upheaval generated by the first two Five-Year Plans, which led to a highly mobile workforce, many non-Jews ended up in the J.A.R. The borders of the J.A.R. were porous and non-Jews willing to settle there without government assistance were welcome.

Thus, it is not surprising that gentiles outnumbered Jews in the purported national homeland of Soviet Jewry. By 1939 Jews accounted for only approximately 18,000 of the some 109,000 residents of the J.A.R.; most Jews (75 percent) lived in the towns and cities. So dismal was the outcome of the campaign to settle Soviet Jewry in the J.A.R. that the number of Jews in the region at the end of the 1930s was far smaller than the number of Russians, Ukrainians, Belarusans, Koreans, Cossacks, and indigenous peoples living there prior to 1928. Semen Dimanshtein offered a realistic assessment of the Jewish presence in the J.A.R. when he wrote in 1934:

We do not set ourselves the goal of establishing quickly a Jewish majority in the Jewish Autonomous Region; we are confident that this will come about as a natural consequence of migration.... Our first task is the expansion and strengthening of socialist construction in the...Jewish Autonomous Region. Therefore, we shall welcome assistance from abroad and non-Jewish cadres as the most important and vital form of help.[8]

FOREIGN SETTLERS AND INTERNATIONAL SUPPORT

The settlement of non-Soviet citizens in the J.A.R. also contributed to the region's growth and underscores the extent to which information about the Birobidzhan project found its way to Europe, North and South America, and South Africa. For example, the J.A.R. received extensive coverage in a 1935 issue of *USSR in Construction*, a profusely illustrated publication that informed English speakers about the achievements of the Soviet Union. From the late 1920s until the mid-1930s, over one thousand foreign Jews moved to the J.A.R. Starting in 1935, all foreigners wishing to settle in the J.A.R. had to pay KOMZET two hundred dollars, which covered all expenses while traveling in the Soviet Union. Many of these Jews had family roots in Russia and were disenchanted with life in Europe and the Americas. They

Birobijan is the Jewish autonomous region which forms part of the Far Eastern Region.

Jewish settlers came from the western and south-western districts of the Soviet Union, from America, Germany, Argentine and other countries to the deserted and impenetrable Siberian forests, to build up a new life entirely different from the life of the old miserable Jewish townlets. They put up their first dwellings — tents — in the forest. Building work began...

Pages 44 through 49: Full-page layouts from a 1935 issue of *USSR in Construction,* a magazine that informed English-language audiences about the achievements of the Soviet Union. 12 × 15 in. (each page).

„I think that the Jewish nationality of Birobijan will not be a nationality with the characteristics of the Jews of the ghettos of Poland, Lithuania, White Russia and even Ukraine, because it is already giving birth to socialist „colonisers" of a free, rich land, to people with big fists and strong teeth, who will be the forebears of a new strong nationality within the family of Soviet peoples"

(from a talk of M. I. Kalinin to a delegation of Moscow workers).

You will not find the shrinking, downtrodden Jews of the ghettos in Birobijan. The people of Birobijan—they are Com. Gefen, the best mower of the Waldheim collective farm (1); Com. Lazar Ugodnikov, the bee-keeper of Birofeld collective farm (2); Com. Serel, manager of the Stalinfeld collective farm (3); Joseph Abramski, the best herdsman of the Inor collective farm (4).

3

2

1

The types of the Jewish ghetto can only be found now on the stage of the Birobijan Jewish theatre.

A group of Argentine Jews
en route to the J.A.R. in 1932.

came especially from Lithuania, Argentina, and the United States and were motivated by a desire to help build socialism and to escape the hardships caused by
the Great Depression. Like many early Zionist pioneers in Palestine, the foreign
Jews who settled in the J.A.R. were attracted by the mystique of tilling the land
and engaging in physical labor. And yet they chose not to go to Palestine and
responded to the propaganda campaigns of pro-Soviet organizations by moving
to the J.A.R., even if not always permanently.

For example, a group of thirty-two Jewish families from the Los Angeles area
sold their homes and businesses and moved to the J.A.R. in the 1930s, only to
return within the year. Grigorii Lerner, a Polish Jew who moved to Argentina
in 1928 and later became head of the Communist Party there, remembers that

Morris and Rose Becker with
their children, Elizabeth and
Mitchell, in Monrovia, California,
about 1930.

two delegations of Argentine Jews moved to the J.A.R. in these years.[9]

In another instance, Morris and Rose Becker of Monrovia, California, chose to emigrate to the J.A.R. in 1931 with their two young children. Morris Becker and his parents had moved to the United States from Russia when he was a young boy, and they earned their living as farmers. After Morris married Rose, who shared her husband's commitment to socialism and Zionism, they moved to California, where they bought farmland and worked for radical causes. According to their daughter, Elizabeth, Rose even served time in jail for her political activities. On hearing about the establishment of Birobidzhan, the Beckers decided to help build socialism in the Jewish homeland of the Soviet Union. Their destination was the ICOR commune, and a surviving member of the commune remembers Rose, who was put in charge of raising pigs, for her fervor and zeal. Rose, who had grown somewhat disillusioned with the J.A.R., died in 1936 from sunstroke, and Morris died shortly thereafter. Elizabeth recalls that her father, whose enthusiasm for the Birobidzhan experiment had soured, was preparing to return to the United States when he died.

The Birobidzhan project was well known among world Jewry. Zionists, representing the sentiments of many Jews in the United States and Europe, actively fought the idea that the J.A.R. satisfied the cultural and national aspirations of Soviet Jewry. However, many prominent Jews outside the Soviet Union

Members of the ICOR commune in 1930, which was composed of many foreign settlers. Formed during the initial years of Jewish settlement, the ICOR commune was disbanded by the end of the 1930s.

In 1932 the Pensacola, Florida, branch of ICOR sent its greetings to the people of the J.A.R. The Yiddish says: "A fiery greeting from Pensacola ICOR to the builders of Birobidzhan."

Cover from the July 1935 issue of *Voice of the Geserd,* a Johannesberg, South Africa, magazine. *Geserd* is the Yiddish acronym for OZET.

In 1936 a delegation from Los Angeles went to the J.A.R., hoping to present this souvenir pamphlet to "the Pioneers of Biro-Bidjan as our Token of Friendship" and place it in the Jewish Museum there. The fate of the delegation is unknown, but one thing is certain: no Jewish Museum existed in the J.A.R. in 1936.

Several hundred people attending a 1938 ICOR meeting in New York.

In March 1938 the Chicago chapter of ICOR published this souvenir program to commemorate the tenth anniversary of Jewish settlement in the J.A.R. The Yiddish at the top reads, "Ten Years of Birobidzhan." The names of settlements in the J.A.R. are written in the streamers held by the hand.

staunchly defended the Kremlin's decision to establish the J.A.R. As the prominent German-Jewish writer Lion Feuchtwanger naively wrote after a brief visit to Moscow in 1937, "The Jewish socialist republic of Birobidzhan is a reality."[10]

In various cities of the world, supporters of the J.A.R. organized committees to publicize awareness of the region and raise funds for it. The most active and significant organization was ICOR (Association for Jewish Colonization in the Soviet Union, or Idishe kolonizatsie organizatsie in Yiddish), which was established in the mid-1920s by pro-Soviet American Jews interested in promoting the agricultural settlement of Jews in the Soviet Union. With the 1928 decision concerning Birobidzhan, ICOR turned its efforts to advertising the movement of Jews to the land in the Soviet Far East. Consisting of some one hundred local committees and over ten thousand dues-paying members by the early 1930s, ICOR raised hundreds of thousands of dollars for the purchase of

ICOR A Magazine published every month (except August) by the Icor,
Ass'n for Jewish Colonization in the Soviet Union, at 799 Broadway, N. Y. C. Tel. STuy. 9-6667

A. ROVNER

GREATEST EVENT IN THE HISTORY OF THE JEWISH PEOPLE

The First Government of the Jewish Autonomous District of Biro Bidjan Will Be Elected on December 11th — Event Will Be Celebrated Throughout the World as Greatest Achiement of Soviet National Policy

On the 11th of December, there will be held in Biro-Bidjan a congress of local Soviets to elect the first government of the Jewish autonomous territory. Besides the local representatives, there are delegates from all the Soviet republics convening in Biro-Bidjan; there are also representatives of Jewish organizations from many countries in the world.

The 11th of December will be celebrated throughout the Soviet Union as a great event. From that day on the Jewish people will be represented in the Government of the Soviet Union as a separate national entity.

The 11th of Dec. marks an important milestone in the great achievements of the Soviet Union in the line of solving the problems of its national minorities. It is a link in the golden chain of accomplishments, which include the liberation of all national minorities, the creation of a possibility for every national minority to build its own culture not only unhampered but with the fullest assistance and cooperation on the part of the Government.

In regard to the Jewish masses the Soviet Government scored the greatest triumph. It inherited millions of Jews who were driven to a life of middlemen. In the course of a few short years these Jews were completely transformed.

700,000 Jews in Soviet Factories

Whereas under the Tzar only 4% of the Jews succeeded in squeezing through the Tzarist restrictions and enter factories, today there are 700,000 Jews in the various Soviet industrial establishments.

350,000 Jews on the Land

The Soviet Government succeeded to carry out a vast project of settling the Jews on the land.

In White Russia, Ukraine and Crimea there are now 350,000 Jewish colonists. The Jewish colonies are completely collectivized and are high-

A New Street in the City of Biro Bidjan

Lead article in *Icor* by A. Rovner about the first elections held after the establishment of the J.A.R. in 1934. The decision to grant autonomous administrative status to the Birobidzhan region signaled the Kremlin's official recognition of the area as the national territory of Soviet Jewry. Supporters of the Soviet Union hailed the formation of the J.A.R. as a sign of the freedom and rights enjoyed by Jews under Communism.

tools and equipment for the fledgling collective farms and factories of the J.A.R. Moreover, ICOR allocated funds for cultural endeavors, such as equipment for printing newspapers, and medical care. ICOR also published a Yiddish-English monthly magazine entitled *Nailebn* (New Life), which lauded the efforts of the Soviet government to provide Soviet Jews with a homeland. ICOR had chapters in parts of Europe and South America, particularly Argentina and Uruguay, where large numbers of Jewish émigrés from Eastern Europe had settled. According to Grigorii Lerner, ICOR had over a thousand members in Argentina, Uruguay, and Chile in the 1930s and 1940s and issued a publication that appeared eleven times a year. Lerner publicized the Birobidzhan ex-

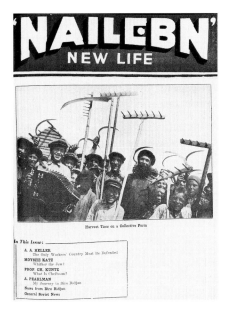

Nailebn (December 1935).

Nailebn (June 1939). Cover illustration by William Gropper. The figure *108,000* refers to the total population of the J.A.R. and not to only Jewish inhabitants, who numbered approximately 18,000 in 1939. The Yiddish word *Forverts* (Forward) is written on the jacket of the man in the bottom left corner. The *Forverts* was the leading Yiddish daily newspaper in the United States in the 1930s. The man, with hands over his eyes, is refusing to acknowledge the reputed success of the J.A.R.

56

Nailebn (November 1937). Note that the man and woman are dressed in typical Russian or Ukrainian peasant garb; the man is dancing a peasant dance.

Nailebn (May 1939). Note the American-style barn and silo, perhaps indicating an American vision of life in the J.A.R.

periment in lectures in Buenos Aires and Montevideo that attracted hundreds of listeners interested in Jewish life in the Soviet Union; he also toured the provinces raising funds and other forms of support for the Soviet Zion.[11]

The material assistance provided by ICOR was supplemented by the largesse of the American Jewish Joint Distribution Committee. In addition, AMBIJAN (American Birobidjan Committee) was active in the 1930s and then again after 1945. Like ICOR, which had close ties to the Communist Party of the United States, AMBIJAN was a Communist front organization, actively recruiting settlers to the J.A.R. and raising funds.

Public support of the J.A.R. was not limited to Jews and their organizations, however. Prominent gentiles also advocated the Birobidzhan project. For example, Lord Marley, a British peer who devoted himself to the Labour Party after his retirement from the navy in 1920, visited the J.A.R. in the fall of 1933.

THE BIROBIDZHAN PROJECT

On his return to England, he published a glowing account of the region, advising that "careful and sympathetic examination should be given to the offer of the Soviet Union to receive persecuted German refugees who are invited to participate in the building up [of] an autonomous Jewish republic in Biro-bidjan."[12]

Similarly, artists in the United States and Europe publicized the J.A.R through their art. At the behest of ICOR, a group of prominent American artists donated over two hundred works of art as a gift to the people of the J.A.R. in 1935. The fruits of their labor were first exhibited in New York and Boston and then arrived in Moscow for display in late 1936. However, the paintings, drawings, and sculptures never found their way to Birobidzhan, their intended final destination. Their fate is unknown.

In 1937 a group of Jewish artists from Chicago celebrated the Birobidzhan experiment by issuing a portfolio of lithographs entitled *A Gift to Biro-bidjhan* in an edition of two hundred. The statement issued by the artists reflected their solidarity with the Jews of the J.A.R. and noted their commitment as artists to help build a more just world: "We, a group of Chicago Jewish artists, in presenting our works to the Builders of Biro-Bidjan—are symbolizing with this action the flowering of a new social concept wherein the artist becomes moulded into the clay of the whole people and becomes the clarion of their hopes and desires.... Thus we will better translate in our media, these aspirations for a new and better life ... to a more understanding world, from our fountain of creation the first sparkling glimpses that are the new Jew in the making." 12 × 15 in.

New Hope by Ceil Rosenberg is reminiscent of Zionist depictions of the modern, secular Jew engaged in physical labor who will replace the traditional, religious Jew. Whereas Zionists looked to Palestine as the site of Jewish renovation, Rosenberg and the other artists who contributed to the portfolio placed their hopes in the J.A.R. From *A Gift to Biro-bidjan.*

West Side by Aaron Bohrod illustrates the disillusionment of the artist with the inability of the U.S. government to deal with the social problems caused by the Great Depression and provides insight into why the Birobidzhan experiment attracted the attention, sympathy, and support of many left-wing Americans. From *A Gift to Biro-bidjan.*

Raisins and Almonds by Todros Geller. Readily available and inexpensive, raisins and almonds were eaten by East European Jews as special treats on holidays and the Sabbath. They were also given as a reward to a young boy when he started to study Torah. From *A Gift to Biro-bidjan.*

CULTURE IN THE J.A.R.

Along with its effort to encourage Jewish migration to the J.A.R., the Soviet government also tried to foster the region's specifically Jewish nature through the use of Yiddish. Yiddish was intended to serve as the bedrock of a secular, proletarian Soviet Jewish culture and community. Paralleling the pronouncements of such Jewish socialists as Chaim Zhitlovsky, the Kremlin pursued the policy of Yiddishism, which posited Yiddish as the basis of the national-cultural consolidation of Soviet Jewry. As the national language of the Jews, Yiddish, rather than Hebrew—which was considered the language of bourgeois Zionists—would help ensure that the cultural politics of Soviet Jewry would hew closely to the dictum, "national in form and socialist in content." According to the architects of the Birobidzhan experiment, the J.A.R. would become the new center of Soviet Jewish life, embodying the principles of Yiddishism and expressing the national sentiments of Soviet Jews. In 1936 the government issued a decree ele-

Student at the Teachers' College in Birobidzhan, mid-1930s. Schools where the language of instruction was Yiddish reinforced the government's emphasis on Yiddish as part of the foundation of Jewish culture in the J.A.R. The bottom book is entitled, in Yiddish, *Lenin*.

vating Yiddish institutions in the J.A.R. to a preeminent position in the Soviet Union. A Yiddish-language conference planned for early 1937 (but never held because of the purges) was "intended to result in the establishment in Birobidzhan of academic and educational institutions empowered to supervise the Yiddish language and Yiddish culture in the Soviet Union."[13]

In 1935 the government decreed that all government documents, including public notices, announcements, posters, and advertisements had to appear in both Yiddish and Russian, even though it is clear that the decree was honored in the breach.[14] Street signs, railway station signs, and postmarks appeared in both Yiddish and Russian, and police and judicial investigations could also be conducted in Yiddish, if the parties involved were Jewish. Jews also served prominently in government and party posts, and the state publicized the "Jew-

Students at the Yiddish elementary school in the village of Londoko, mid-1930s.

Students attending a Korean school in the village of Blagoslavennyi, 1936. The region designated for Jewish settlement in 1928 was inhabited by Great Russians, Cossacks, Koreans, and Ukrainians who had moved there in the late nineteenth and early twentieth centuries. In the mid-1930s some 4,500 Koreans lived in the J.A.R. and, like the Jews, were entitled to attend schools where classes were conducted in their national language.

ish" coloration of social, cultural, and political life in the J.A.R. In addition, a variety of Yiddish cultural institutions, including a newspaper and a library with a sizable Judaica collection, were established. The Jewish Theater named after Lazar Kaganovich, a Jew who was a trusted aide of Stalin, opened in 1934 when members of the Moscow State Jewish Theater arrived in the J.A.R. along with musicians, technical personnel, and costumes. Its first show was an adaptation of a Sholem Aleichem story, and, in addition to performing for the residents of the J.A.R., the troupe also toured the Soviet Far East. The government also set up schools in which Yiddish was the language of instruction, and Yiddish became an obligatory subject in schools where classes were conducted in Russian.

Well-known Yiddish writers and Jewish intellectuals visited the J.A.R. in the 1930s and affirmed the official line that the Birobidzhan project embodied the national and cultural aspirations of Soviet Jewry. For example, in 1932 the Yiddish writer David Bergelson visited Birobidzhan and participated in a literary club, which served as a gathering place and source of inspiration for Jewish

The Jewish Theater,
which opened in 1934.

writers. When the Yiddish literary journal *Forpost* (Outpost) began to appear in 1936, critics hailed it as an important Soviet-Jewish journal, which "should be the central organ of not only local Birobidzhan forces, but of all creative forces of Soviet Jewish society interested in the construction of the Jewish Autonomous Region."[15] At other times, the use of Yiddish was clearly intended for propaganda purposes, as in 1936 when Kaganovich visited the J.A.R. and attended a party conference where he and other officials gave parts of their speeches in Yiddish.

It must be remembered, however, that the political climate in the 1930s required writers to tailor their work to fit the uniform ideological mold established by the regime. In the early 1930s the editors of the *Birobidzhaner shtern*, the Yiddish daily in the J.A.R. since 1930, organized a group of Jewish proletarian writers whose aim was to illustrate the benefits of Soviet power to Jews and "reflect in Jewish literature the socialist construction of Birobidzhan," particularly the fulfilling and overfulfilling of the Five-Year Plans among workers and collective farmers.[16] As far as they were concerned, Soviet Jewish culture served the interests of the regime by celebrating the achievements of

Members of the Yiddish literary
club in the early 1930s.

Stalin, of Five-Year Plans, and of socialist construction. Literary efforts focused on the transformation of Soviet Jews into productive citizens who labored in the collective and state farms and factories that began to dot the landscape of the J.A.R. Taming the harsh taiga, contributing to the building of socialism in the Soviet Far East, and "laying the foundation for a new, multifaceted Jewish culture" were the themes deemed worthy by the Kremlin.[17]

In contrast to the stultifying religious environment and grinding poverty of the shtetl, the J.A.R. signaled the dawn of a new age for Jews, an age in which Soviet Jews would express contempt for Jewish tradition, free themselves of the burdens, limitations, and prejudices of the past, and glorify Soviet power as they became integral members of the socialist society under construction. Two Yiddish novels, by David Bergelson (*Birobidzhaner*) and M. Alberton (*Birobidzhan*), published soon after the beginning of Jewish settlement, illustrate this literary emphasis on the J.A.R. as the embodiment of Jewish life; in the words of one reviewer, the works portray the "first steps of Jewish settlers" to the new center of Jewish society.[18]

The Yiddish newspaper *Birobidzhaner shtern* first appeared in 1930 and has been published (except for a few years during World War II) on a regular basis. This is the edition for July 24, 1931. It is one of the few Yiddish newspapers still published in the world today.

Yiddish schools in the J.A.R. reinforced this emphasis on socialist construction. As of 1937, sixteen schools existed, with close to two thousand students, and all subjects, including the natural sciences and math, were taught in Yiddish. Indeed, a Yiddish version of a school text on the geography and economic resources of the J.A.R. appeared even before the Russian-language text did. Not surprisingly, these schools followed the lead of other Yiddish schools in Belarus and Ukraine by turning their back on traditional Jewish education, with its focus on religion and Hebrew. Instead, the Jewish content of these schools was heavily laden with propaganda and designed to instill feelings of Soviet patriotism and loyalty to Stalin and his policies. Courses on Jewish literature included texts by Sholom Aleichem and Mendele Mokher Sforim because of their focus on the Jewish poor and depictions of impoverished shtetl life. In turn, courses on Jewish history stressed class struggle and the exploitation of the Jewish poor by Jewish communal institutions controlled by rabbis and wealthy Jews. Yet as Zvi Gitelman observes about Yiddish schools in Ukraine and Belarus in the 1920s, they "differed from the general schools in form and not in substance. . . . Of course, it was not only *Jewish* history which was distorted almost beyond recognition. . . . Imprisoned by its own ideology and preconceptions, the Communist Party . . . had an extremely limited area in which to experiment with the creation of a Soviet Jewish culture and a Soviet Yiddish educational system."[19]

To be able to live in a region devoted specifically to their cultural needs undoubtedly attracted many Soviet Jews to the J.A.R. Not all heard the call, however. As one woman who grew up in Gomel, Belarus, remembered, "Gomel was a real Jewish city . . . and so in that sense we felt as if everything was ours. . . . We didn't have to think about going to Birobidzhan."[20] One person who felt the lure of the J.A.R., however, was Isaac Prishkol'nik, who went to Waldheim in the mid-1930s as a teenager precisely because its status as the proclaimed center of Soviet Jewry appealed to his commitment to Yiddish. Prishkol'nik, who still spoke Yiddish with his wife and some of his neighbors in the early 1990s, noted that Waldheim in the 1930s compared favorably to Smolensk, his hometown west of Moscow. Not only was "Yiddish spoken everywhere" when he arrived, but he did not experience anti-Semitism and felt "more comfortable" in Waldheim than in Smolensk.[21] Fira Kofman, another longtime resident of the J.A.R., arrived in Birobidzhan in 1936. Like Prishkol'nik, Kofman was an enthusiastic teenage member of the Young Communist League who responded to the government's appeal to move to the J.A.R. and help build a socialist homeland for Soviet Jewry. As she recalled in 1994, Birobidzhan possessed a distinctive Jewish air. "Yiddish was heard on the streets. . . . We had Jewish schools, a Jewish theater, a Jewish restaurant where one could eat real Jewish food. . . . So, one could feel the Jewish atmosphere. Why not? This is, after all, the Jewish Autonomous Region."[22] Both Prishkol'nik and Kofman fondly remembered their years as young adults in the J.A.R. of the 1930s precisely because they believed that their hopes, dreams, and expectations as young Communists and Jews were fulfilled by living in the Soviet Zion. As the lives of Prishkol'nik and Kofman illustrate, the Kremlin's efforts to establish a Jewish homeland drew sustenance from such popular impulses.

Officials in the J.A.R. actively combated religious practices among Jews. Though the existing sources make it difficult to assess the extent of religious observance in the J.A.R. in the 1930s, it is clear that some Jews did practice their religion, including the baking of matza for Passover. During his 1930 visit to the J.A.R., Otto Heller, the prominent German Communist, noted the existence of a makeshift prayer house made of mud and grass. Similarly, other visitors to the region in the early 1930s stated that Jewish settlers observed Rosh Hashanah and Yom Kippur. In 1937 a group of Jews, including one man who had brought a Torah to Birobidzhan, set up a *minyan*, which was a nonregistered and unofficial assembly that met and prayed on the Sabbath and Jewish holidays in a private apartment in lieu of a synagogue. At Passover time, however, a series of lectures and other events were held in factories and workers' clubs to undercut the appeal of Judaism. Organized by the regional League of the Militant Godless, the lectures covered a range of topics such as the incompatibility of socialism and religion. Moreover, they specifically targeted women, who were seen as the bulwark of religious belief and practices in the Jewish family. Given the absence of a synagogue and the prevailing political climate, which made open religious observance risky, the antireligion campaigns enjoyed no small degree of success as Jews found it difficult to practice their religion.

The true nature of relations between Jews and non-Jews is also difficult to determine. Even though officials tended to gloss over anti-Semitic incidents and went out of their way to proclaim the solidarity and friendship among the various nationalities of the J.A.R., at times they did publicize the occurrence of anti-Semitic acts. In 1931 government and party leaders noted that "decent relations" among Jews, Russians, Ukrainians, and Koreans existed, but they also reported an increasing number of "incidents of an anti-Semitic nature," which they attributed to peasants who opposed collectivization and other class enemies working on state farms and in construction. The officials undertook educational efforts to undermine "Great Power chauvinism," the standard way of referring to excessive Russian national pride and patriotism. They claimed this attitude contributed to both anti-Semitism and anti-Asian sentiments and had

In an effort to combat religious observance among Jews, the leadership of the J.A.R. organized an antireligion campaign. This poster from about 1937 lists a series of lectures and other events that were held in factories and workers' clubs throughout the J.A.R. at Passover time. The titles of some of the lectures given to schoolchildren and factory workers were "The Class Nature of Passover," "The Struggle against Religion, the Struggle for Socialism," and "The Woman in the Front Ranks of Militant Atheists." 14 × 22 in.

"deep roots in daily life and at work and . . . is hidden and hard to see." They also insisted that Russians were not the only guilty parties in sowing the seeds of national hatred. Koreans living in the J.A.R., officials claimed, displayed a strong dislike of Russian, Ukrainian, and Jewish inhabitants of the region.[23]

To some extent, newspaper accounts reveal the frequency with which anti-Semitism reared its head in the region during the 1930s. Generally speaking, the guilty parties were uneducated Russians and Ukrainians who, after having too much to drink, targeted Jews for anti-Semitic name-calling, Jew-baiting, and at times physical assault with fists, knives, and guns. Yet in some cases, the anti-Semites were looking for a scapegoat and blamed Jews for problems on the collective farms and in industrial enterprises. In one instance, a Russian vented his anger at being coerced into joining a collective farm by stating that he resents being told what to do by "kikes."[24] In another case, a Ukrainian shouted in a store in Birobidzhan, "I will slaughter all the Jews. I can't stand them."[25]

Whatever the motivations of the anti-Semites, local authorities vigorously prosecuted anti-Semitic behavior and showed no leniency. In April 1935 a Russian machinist at a railway depot was sentenced to five years in prison for a series of nasty pranks he played on Jewish co-workers.[26] And in 1937 two construction workers who had drinking problems and made anti-Semitic slurs in their dormitory were sentenced to two years in prison.[27]

THE GREAT TERROR
AND THE END OF THE
BIROBIDZHAN PROJECT

The inhabitants of the J.A.R. did not escape the bloodletting of the purges unleashed by Stalin and the secret police between 1936 and 1938. The purges served several purposes, not the least of which was the consolidation of Stalin's grip on the party and government. They also helped to affix blame on scapegoats for the failings of the Five-Year Plans and to mobilize support for the policies of the Kremlin in its struggle against supposed enemies. Though the precise number of persons arrested, executed, and sent to the burgeoning labor-camp system, where many died from exhaustion, malnutrition, and disease, is not known, reliable estimates indicate that several million Soviet citizens—and perhaps thousands in the J.A.R.—fell victim to the maelstrom of the purges in these years.

In the J.A.R., during the course of two days in September 1937, the security forces deported the region's 4,500 Koreans in sealed freight trains to Central Asia. Similarly, the political leadership of the region was hard hit by arrests and executions. Lazar Kaganovich played an active role as one of Stalin's chief henchmen. Prominent Jewish officials such as the government head Iosif Liberberg (former head of the Institute for Jewish Proletarian Culture in Kiev) and the party leader Matvei Khavkin were accused of counterrevolutionary activities, including "bourgeois nationalism" and Trotskyism. These men, along with their assistants, were targeted not because they were Jewish but because they had become politically suspect due to their involvement in Jewish causes. In Liberberg's case, the purge commission ironically accused him of attempting to establish the J.A.R. as the center of Jewish culture in the Soviet Union. Khavkin was arrested in 1937 and languished in prison until January 1941 when, after three military tribunals, he was sentenced to fifteen years in the gulag. By this time a series of interrogators had subjected him to countless beatings, which resulted in a loss of several teeth and an injury to his spine. Khavkin managed to survive the rigors of camp life and subsequent exile un-

Death certificate of Nikolai Blagoi, head of the Young Communist League in the J.A.R. The secret police arrested Blagoi in 1938. The document states, "Top Secret... Sentence regarding the shooting of Nikolai Blagoi has been carried out in Khabarovsk, May 25, 1938."

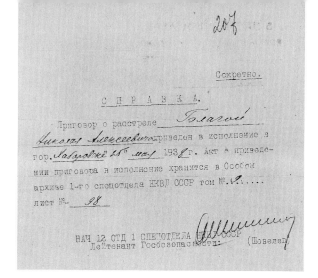

til 1956 when, in the wake of Nikita Khrushchev's de-Stalinization campaign, the Kremlin overturned his sentence and permitted him to return to Moscow. Khavkin's wife, Sofia, also fell victim to the secret police who accused her of trying to poison Kaganovich with homemade gefilte fish during his 1936 visit to the J.A.R. She was arrested along with her husband, sentenced to a labor camp, and tragically ended up in a mental hospital.

Though other Jews frequently replaced the Jews who were purged, the shake-up of government and party personnel signaled the end of the Kremlin's efforts to devote significant resources and attention to the J.A.R. Both OZET and KOMZET were disbanded during the purges, and prominent Kremlin advocates of the Birobidzhan project, including Semen Dimanshtein, were imprisoned or executed.

By the late 1930s Stalin's emphasis on Great Russian patriotism had come to the fore, and policies designed to facilitate the cultural expression of various

Lazar Kaganovich

Iosif Liberberg

Matvei Khavkin

national and ethnoreligious minorities fell by the wayside. The state closed virtually all the Yiddish schools in the J.A.R. as well as elsewhere in the Soviet
Union. In this regard, the Jews of the J.A.R. were not singled out for special
treatment, since the government also clamped down on cultural and educational institutions of national minorities both in and out of their respective territorial enclaves. The division of the pedagogical college, which trained teachers for Jewish schools, was dismantled, as were all institutions dealing with
Jewish land settlement. By 1941 only two Jewish schools were still in operation,
a high school in Birobidzhan and an elementary school in nearby Waldheim.
The concerted effort to stimulate Jewish migration to the region had ended.

An additional curiosity in this often self-contradictory enterprise remains.
Despite this onslaught on the J.A.R., the Kremlin, presumably for propaganda
purposes, did not destroy the institutional and legal foundation of the region
as it did in the territorial enclaves of many other national minorities. By
1939–40 the Soviet annexation of eastern Poland, the Baltic countries, and
parts of Romania gave rise to a plan to transfer part of the Jewish population
in those regions to the J.A.R. However, the outbreak of hostilities with Germany in June 1941 halted the plan's implementation. By the eve of World War
II most non-Soviet observers concluded that the Birobidzhan project was an ab-
ject failure; the fact that Jews accounted for just 16 percent (17,695 of approximately 109,000 inhabitants) of the J.A.R.'s population in 1939 is stark evidence
of the inability of the government to build a genuinely Jewish region in the
Soviet Far East.

Thus, the J.A.R. never lived up to the goals of its proponents to become a center of Soviet Jewry embodying the aspirations of a secular, Yiddishist culture.
By the mid-1930s, notwithstanding the lip service paid by Soviet officialdom
to the region, the intent of Soviet nationality policy was to efface Jewish national identity in the long run with the growth of Soviet socialism. Assimilation into the emerging Soviet way of life—the development of *homo sovieticus*
—rather than the blossoming of Jewish national identity, became an overrid-
ing goal of the Communist Party. The Kremlin desired the fusion of all national cultures into a common socialist culture with the Russian language as
the glue.[28]

The irony is that as Soviet Jewry achieved the semblance of national-cultural
consolidation, little was left of the specifically Jewish content of the culture in
the territory; the government aimed at stripping the region of all traditional
manifestations of Jewish culture. The policy of "national in form and socialist in content" had reduced culture and national identity to language, while im-
posing strict limits on content. For most government and party officials, however, the existence of a Jewish territorial enclave in the Soviet Union (as

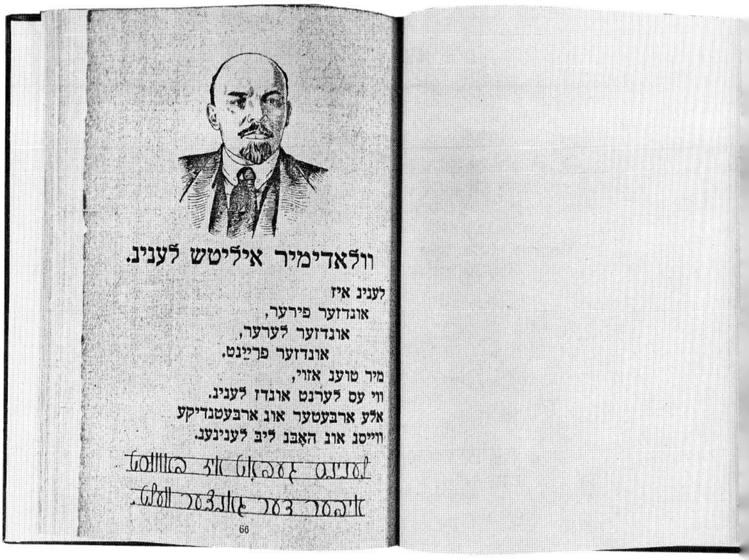

וולאדימיר איליטש לענין.

לענין איז
אונדזער פירער,
אונדזער לערער,
אונדזער פרײַנט.
מיר טוען אזוי,
ווי עס לערנט אונדז לענין.
אלע ארבעטער און ארבעטנדיקע
ווייסן און האָבן ליב לענינען.

66

This elementary school primer from 1936 illustrates how the classroom curriculum served the needs of the Kremlin by fulfilling the dictum, "national in form and socialist in content." 9 × 13 in. (open).

opposed to the stirrings of Jewish settlement in Palestine, to which emigration was closed off by the 1930s) was sufficient evidence of the Kremlin's successful policy toward Soviet Jewry.

The public assertion that the J.A.R. had become the center of Soviet Jewish life and culture satisfied the desires of most government and party officials, who were, after all, more interested in the form than the content of the socialist Zion. How, indeed, did the publication of books written in Yiddish about the exploits of Lenin further the development of Jewish culture? A case in point is the following excerpt from the 1936 Yiddish school primer shown above:

Vladimir Ilich Lenin
Lenin is our leader,
Our teacher, our friend
We do as Lenin teaches us,
All working people know and love Lenin.

Such a book may have helped schoolchildren learn Yiddish, but its contribution to the transmission of Jewish culture and traditions was dubious to say the least. As Lucy Dawidowicz notes in her memoir, "Yiddish was an insufficient basis on which to maintain one's identity."[29] Although Dawidowicz is specifically referring to Jewish life in Vilna, Lithuania, during the 1930s, where circumstances were more conducive to Jewish life than in the Soviet Union, her realization also applies to the fate of Jews in the J.A.R. Reliance on Yiddish alone could not safeguard Jewish cultural identity, especially when a host of factors was at work to undermine the appeal and force of the language.

Socioeconomic, cultural, and political developments scuttled the experiment in Jewish territorialization and Yiddishism. Responsibility for the failure of Birobidzhan does not belong solely to the Kremlin. Even if the government had taken its commitment to the J.A.R. more seriously, it is likely that the effort to establish a socialist Zion within the borders of the Soviet Union would have failed. By the mid-1930s Jews seeking escape from the dead-end world of the shtetl had other avenues for social and economic advancement than migration to the J.A.R. Since the abolition of the Pale of Settlement and the establishment of Communist rule, hundreds of thousands of shtetl Jews had been flocking to the cities of the Russian heartland, a process accelerated during the crash industrialization of the 1930s, which brought opportunities in education, government employment, technical and vocational training, and factory work. Why would a Jew from a shtetl in Belarus or Ukraine choose to move to the J.A.R. when a new life beckoned in Kiev, Moscow, Odessa, or Leningrad, cities that boasted rich cultural offerings and well-established Jewish populations, not to mention myriad work opportunities? Moreover, reliance on Yiddish, which never enjoyed the prestige of Russian, limited the prospects and opportunities for Soviet Jews who nevertheless needed to learn Russian to succeed in Stalin's Russia. Why attend Yiddish schools when Russian was the language necessary for professional success and advancement? Opportunities for upward mobility abounded in Stalin's Russia, but Yiddish and the J.A.R. did not figure prominently in the minds of those seeking to get ahead. As one American observer of the J.A.R. noted in 1938, "[I]f national culture is simply a linguistic variation of something which is called 'general Soviet culture,' then why does one have to have it? The young Jew is well able to learn Russian."[30] Thus, acculturation to Russian was virtually inevitable given government policy, personal preferences, and socioeconomic developments.

SECOND WIND:
THE POSTWAR
REVIVAL

Ironically, the trauma of World War II breathed life again into the J.A.R., as it did into Soviet Jewish society in general. The war years had witnessed the continuation of prewar trends in the region, with Jewish cultural life remaining at a standstill. With the exception of two schools, all Yiddish schools remained closed, as did the Jewish department at the Teachers' College. The *Birobidzhaner shtern,* the Yiddish daily that had been appearing since 1930, ceased publication between the fall of 1941 and 1944. The end of hostilities in 1945, however, saw the revival of Jewish migration to the region. Not only did tens of thousands of Soviet Jews find themselves displaced by the devastation wrought by the Germans, but many Jews returning to their homes sometimes faced hostile welcomes from their Ukrainian and Belarusan neighbors. These domestic factors worked in tandem with the desire to divert Soviet Jewry's attention away from Palestine in order to generate a renewal of Jewish immigration to the J.A.R. Between 1946 and 1948 perhaps as many as ten thousand Jews moved to the J.A.R., with many settling on collective and state farms as unskilled laborers and skilled professionals such as engineers, technicians, agronomists, and teachers. By the end of 1948 estimates indicate that as many as thirty thousand Jews were living in the region; many hoped that the J.A.R. would be elevated to the status of autonomous republic. In the words of one prominent Soviet Jewish cultural figure speaking in 1948 to score propaganda points in the United States, "post-war immigration to Birobidzhan has exceeded all expectations. If this immigration continues at the present rate, an autonomous Socialist Soviet Jewish Republic will be set up in the Far East in a few years."[31] And Mikhail Kalinin continued his public support of the J.A.R. when he stated in 1948 that he considered the region "a Jewish national state" that will "regenerate" Soviet Jews through "creative toil."[32]

Official efforts to resuscitate Jewish migration to the J.A.R. began soon after the end of the war. In early 1946 the Council of Ministers announced a plan to stimulate the development of the region. As in the 1930s, the goals of populating and developing the Soviet Far East were also behind the government's actions regarding the J.A.R. The plan focused on the building of industrial enterprises and the construction of new apartment houses and decreed that professionals such as medical doctors, teachers, and agronomists be sent to the J.A.R. The government also offered free transportation, a loan, and other incentives to those settlers who chose to till the land. Articles about the J.A.R. saturated the pages of the remaining Soviet Jewish press, and delegations of representatives from the region toured the towns and villages of Belarus and Ukraine as part of the concerted recruitment drive. As one Jewish woman recounted about her move from the Caucasus to Waldheim in these years,

In October 1947 my husband brought home a newspaper with an article 'The Far East Appeals for New Settlers.' Semyon talked me into it as well as several other families belonging to our collective farm. The state paid our travelling expenses, gave us money for food and other expenditures along the way besides a large sum of money on long-term credit so that we could begin building when we arrived at our new home.[33]

Government official greeting new Jewish settlers in 1948. As in the early years of Jewish settlement, the government again offered free transportation and other material incentives to Jews who went to the J.A.R. Special train convoys, such as the one pictured here, brought thousands of Jewish settlers who were met with great fanfare.

By the end of 1946 the first wave of Jewish migrants had boarded special trains destined for the J.A.R.; over the course of the next eighteen months, a dozen or so of these trains, carrying over six thousand Jewish settlers, arrived in the region. They were met with great fanfare and their journey was publicized both at home and abroad in a variety of publications. They supplemented the several thousand other migrants, both Jews and gentiles, who also had chosen to move to the J.A.R. after the war. In the summer of 1947 the well-known Yiddish writer Der Nister traveled with an echelon of Jewish settlers. After spending several weeks in Birobidzhan, he returned to Moscow, where he publicized the efforts to revive Jewish life and culture.

Many Jews responded to the appeal and moved to the J.A.R., viewing the region as a land of opportunity and a way to escape the war-ravaged conditions of the western Soviet Union. Personal loss and a sense of tragedy motivated many prospective migrants to seek new lives in a new venue. A Jewish woman from Moldava described why she wanted to move to the J.A.R.: "I am a seam-

בּיראָבּידזשאַן

אַלמאַנאַך

1(4)

Cover of the *Birobidzhan
almanakh,* a journal that reflected
the revival of the Birobidzhan
project.

stress who lost all my relatives in the war. Only two nephews remain and they
plan to move to Birobidzhan after demobilization."[34] That the J.A.R. was
officially reserved for Jewish settlement undoubtedly added to the lure of the
place.[35] As one couple from Vinnitsa reported, they had come to the J.A.R. to
"help build Jewish Soviet statehood." Similarly, two other Jewish settlers proclaimed at a reception celebrating their arrival that they had not "come as
guests but had come home. Long live our native home."[36]

This concerted effort to populate the J.A.R. with Jews occurred as the Kremlin briefly relaxed its grip on Soviet society, a process begun during the war
years. A resurgence of Jewish cultural life followed. With the approval of the
Kremlin, J.A.R. party chief Aleksandr Bakhmutskii spearheaded a drive to revive the use of Yiddish in the region. Given the significant number of Jews living in the region, the party organization in the J.A.R. was instructed to "pay
more attention to party propaganda in Yiddish" and to deliver "more speeches
in Yiddish."[37] Although most Jews in the J.A.R. undoubtedly understood Russian, the party believed that the national language of the region, Yiddish,
merited propaganda and advocacy. In addition, the Communist Party ordered
the increased circulation of the *Birobidzhaner shtern,* stressing that more
efforts be taken to expand the number of subscribers to the Yiddish newspaper. It also insisted that electoral lists to the local soviets be published in both
Yiddish and Russian. Finally, the government opened a Yiddish publishing
house for books, periodicals, and textbooks, leading to the appearance of several issues of the *Birobidzhan almanakh,* a literary and cultural journal, from
1946 to 1948, to replace the defunct *Forpost.* Yiddish once again became an
obligatory subject in schools, including those where Russian was the language
of instruction. Nowhere else in the Soviet Union did this occur.

Yet the number of students attending the two remaining all-Yiddish schools
did not exceed 250 by the end of 1947. The Jewish high school saw its num-

ber of students drop from 497 in 1938–39 to 111 during the 1946–47 school year. Clearly, the vast majority of Jewish youths in the J.A.R., many of whom may have spoken Yiddish at home but Russian elsewhere, realized that receiving an all-Yiddish education made little sense when all forms of higher education and employment were conducted in Russian. As one observer of the Yiddish scene in the J.A.R. pessimistically noted, "Many party activists realize there is not much of a future for Yiddish." Nevertheless, they proclaimed, "If we won't have any Jewish schools or Jewish newspapers, then what will remain Jewish in the J.A.R.?"[38]

A revival of Yiddish literary ventures organized by a group of energetic and enthusiastic novelists, dramatists, and poets also took place under the direction of Boris (Buzi) Miller (editor of the *Birobidzhaner shtern* from the late 1930s until 1947), Liuba Wasserman, Ber Slutskii, and Israel Emiot. The Jewish Theater expanded its activity and even performed plays about the Holocaust. As the actor A. F. Gel'fand noted at a party conference in 1947, the J.A.R. "exists so that Jewish people could create in its native language a culture socialist in content."[39]

Moreover, in May 1946, as part of the commemoration of the thirtieth anniversary of Sholom Aleichem's death, a major thoroughfare of Birobidzhan was renamed in his honor. Lectures, discussions, concerts, and other events were held throughout the region lauding the renowned Yiddish writer. In addition, one wing of the regional museum, which had opened in 1945, was devoted to Jewish history and culture since antiquity. As an article in the *Birobidzhanskaia zvezda* (The Birobidzhan Star) noted, the museum is not only about the history of the J.A.R. but is "also a museum about the Jews . . . which

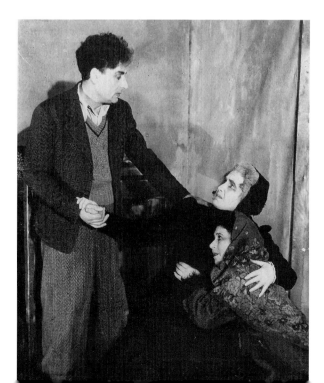

Scene from a performance of *Uprising in the Ghetto,* by the Jewish Theater, in the years following World War II.

should reflect the culture and way of life of the Jewish laboring masses in the Soviet Union."[40] At the behest of Bakhmutskii, the director of the museum was negotiating the transfer to Birobidzhan of the remaining collection of Judaica from the Odessa city museum as well as materials from the Museum of Ethnography in Leningrad and the Moscow State Museum of Art.

Despite this revival in Jewish culture, artists and writers were confined by the ideological straitjacket constraining them since the 1930s. The output of Jewish artists and writers was subject to the same state impositions as others, though there was, in the words of Yehoshua Gilboa, a short-lived "national awakening" in Soviet Jewish culture at this time.[41] The caution and reserve exhibited during the bloodletting of the 1930s fell only partially to the wayside after the Germans had been vanquished and the government had relaxed its grip on society, albeit temporarily. Still, artists and writers had to tread carefully, ever fearful of transgressing the bounds of the politically acceptable.

As part of this "national awakening," Soviet officials encouraged Yiddish authors to write about the valiant contribution of Soviet Jews to the victory over the Germans and the building socialism in the Soviet Far East. Thus, those authors found themselves writing odes to the efforts of the original Jewish settlers to clear the forests, drain the swamps, and erect the factories of the J.A.R. A public competition for a "Soviet-Jewish song to mark the thirtieth anniversary" of the Bolshevik seizure of power stated that the music and lyrics of the winning song "must reflect 1) the basic socioeconomic changes that have taken place in the life of the Jewish people during the years of Soviet power; 2) the

Religious items from the Jewish Division of the Historical Museum of the J.A.R. in 1948.

active participation of Jewish toilers in socialist construction and defense of the homeland; 3) the construction of Soviet Jewish statehood; and 4) the boundless loyalty of Jewish toilers to the Bolshevik Party and the Great Stalin." The guidelines of the competition also listed examples of possible themes, such as "Comrade Stalin—Great Leader and Friend of the People" and "Jews as Stakhanovites in Industry, Transport, and Agriculture."[42]

Also noteworthy were paintings and drawings by artists that were lauded as exemplars of the flourishing of Jewish culture in the J.A.R. In the best socialist-realist fashion, the titles of these works included *The Brigadier in the Field, Meeting of Brigadiers, Where Once There Was Taiga, Socialist Town,* and *Portrait of a Young Tractor Driver.* In fact, the only aspect of these paintings that is particularly Jewish is the artists themselves, who happen to be Jews. The same applies to Shifra Kochina's 1946 Yiddish story "How We Achieve Large Vegetable Crops" and to most of the literary output from the J.A.R.: the authors were Jews and wrote in Yiddish, but there is no specifically Jewish theme or content except for the fact that they are populated by Jews who live in the J.A.R., the purported center of the new Soviet Jewish man and woman. Virtually nothing distinguishes these stories from similar ones written in the languages of other national minorities.

Yet it is clear that not all Jewish inhabitants of the J.A.R. had left behind their Jewish traditions, values, and commitments, including religious observance. Abetted by the Kremlin's relaxation of the strictures against organized religion that had begun during the war, religious life in the region experienced a brief revival. In late 1946 the Council for the Affairs of Religious Cults approved a petition submitted by Jews in Birobidzhan to open a synagogue. Interestingly, the officials who approved the petition stated that the synagogue had been "active" before the war. Since no synagogue had existed in the 1930s, the council was evidently referring to the unofficial gatherings of Jews who met to observe various Jewish holidays in private apartments and makeshift prayer houses. With no rabbi and only a cantor, the Birobidzhan synagogue was the only registered synagogue in that part of the Soviet Far East and received a Torah donated by the Jewish community of Irkutsk. The secret police noted that the city government had helped repair the building that became the synagogue, using funds originally allocated for the repair of schools.[43]

With characteristic ambivalence, however, party officials expressed alarm that in 1947 some four to five hundred persons, including army officers and policemen in uniform, attended High Holiday services. This participation prompted the officials to note that the management of several factories and even some party leaders in Birobidzhan had not taken adequate measures to counteract the influence Judaism still had on many Jews. In general, the au-

RESOLUTIONS OF NATIONAL COMMITTEE

AMBIJAN BULLETIN

VOL. VIII, No. I   15 CENTS   JANUARY-FEBRUARY, 1949

GROUP OF BIROBIDJAN YIDDISH WRITERS: MILLER, SLOTZKY, FRIEDMAN, BRAUNFMAN, LUBA WASSERMAN, RABINKOV, KERLER AND BORJES.

Cover of *Ambijan Bulletin* (January–February 1949). The writers pictured here formed the core of the postwar Yiddish literary revival in the J.A.R. Among those pictured are Boris Miller, Liuba Wasserman, Ber Slutsky, and Hershel Rabinkov.

thorities were upset with the upsurge in religious activities and organizations, including illegal churches, in the J.A.R. Of particular concern were the many workers of all ages, from a variety of enterprises, who preferred synagogue to work on Rosh Hashanah and Yom Kippur. Even more galling was the fact that the elderly parents of several prominent party officials went to synagogue, obviously not feeling any compunction about their actions. As the head of the secret police suggested in early 1948, "I am not advocating the use of repression, but it is imperative to pull our workers out from under the influence" of the synagogue and religious Jews.[44]

The government thus redoubled its antireligious propaganda and pressured many people who were official members of the Jewish community (*obshchina*) to resign their positions. Whereas in 1947, 300 Jews belonged to the *obshchina*, only 43 did the following year. In 1948 many Jews chose to go to the theater or movies rather than attend High Holiday services at the synagogue. Nonetheless, despite this success from the perspective of the party, many Jews continued to observe their religion, with some 300 Jews attending such services in 1950.

Moreover, as in the 1930s, the international Jewish community rallied to the support of the J.A.R. AMBIJAN redoubled its publicity campaign, and similar organizations throughout the world helped raise funds for the J.A.R., sending food, clothing, and machinery. Between 1945 and 1948 some six million rubles'

Flyers publicizing concerts organized by ICOR and AMBIJAN to raise funds for the J.A.R. and to celebrate the twentieth anniversary of Jewish settlement there. Prominent Jewish actors, musicians, and singers lent their talents to these events.

AMBIJAN brochure from about 1947 publicizing the J.A.R., particularly efforts to resettle children orphaned by the war. The figure of 25,000 new Jewish settlers since 1945 is clearly an exaggeration. No more than 100 orphans found their way to the J.A.R. In the last paragraph of the pamphlet, the author erroneously states that Jews make up the majority of the 185,000 inhabitants of the J.A.R.

Wedding in Birobidzhan,
illustration by Marc Chagall, 1944.
Chagall made this drawing to
illustrate the poem by the well-
known Soviet Yiddish poet Itsik
Fefer. Along with many other
prominent Yiddish writers, Fefer
was arrested in the late 1940s
and executed in 1952.

worth of food and supplies reached the J.A.R. from organizations in the United States. AMBIJAN also stressed the need to resettle Jewish children orphaned by the war, though perhaps no more than a hundred orphans found homes in the J.A.R. The support offered by prominent public figures such as Albert Einstein, who served as honorary president, lent AMBIJAN further credibility and a high profile. Once again it seemed as if the J.A.R. might fulfill its role as the Soviet Zion.

Despite the renewed attention and devotion of resources to the J.A.R., many of the same problems that had beset local officials in the 1930s continued to

Birobidyán

Año III   N° 8

BOLETIN INFORMATIVO
SOBRE LA REGION AUTONOMA ISRAELITA EN LA UNION SOVIETICA

Redacción y Administración: CHARRUA 1827   Montevideo, FEBRERO de 1950

ייִדישע באַנק אין אורוגוויי

אין די אינציקע ייִדישע פֿאָלקס־באַנק פֿון אונדזער ייִשעװ

באַ'מעלאָבע: סויכער אין אינדוסטריאַל:

אַרבעטער:

פֿאַרזיכער דײַן עקאָנאָמישע עקזיסטענץ אין הײַלע ליון די קאָאָפּעראַטיװע פֿאַרבינדמען פֿון אונדזער ייִשעװ

א) פֿיר דורך אַלע עקאָנאָמישע אין דער ייִדישער באַנק
ב) פֿראַגע אַרײַן דיינע עקאָנאָמישע פֿראַגעס אין דיין פֿ' ..
נאַציאָנעלע אינסטיטוציע.
ג) גיב אַריבער דער ייִדישער באַנק ראַם פֿאַזיכורי דייִנט
ד) צאַל מיט כעקעס פֿון דער ייִדישער באַנק.

הײַם אַף דיינע אייניגע אונטערגעס מיט דער ייִדישער באַנק

BANCO ISRAELITA DEL URUGUAY

25 DE MAYO 684   TELEFS.: 9.28.72 y 9.28.82

EPU* Aniversario de **LENIN**

LENIN - Esbozo biográfico del Inst. Marx, Engels, Lenin de Moscú
(encuadernación de lujo). Edición Problemas .... $ 1.50
LENIN - Obras Escogidas
4volúmenes - Edición Problemas Cada volúmen .... $ 1.—
HISTORIA DEL PARTIDO COMUNISTA DE LA U.R.S.S.
Encuadernación de lujo. Edición Problemas .... $ 1.—
CUESTIONES DEL LENINISMO - Stalin
Complemento indispensable de las Obras Escogidas de Lenin y de la
Historia del Partido. Edición Problemas .... $ 1.—
EL MARXISMO Y EL PROBLEMA NACIONAL Y COLONIAL - Stalin
Edición Lautaro .... $ 1.—

Adquiéralos en **LIBRERIA E. P. U.**

COLONIA y TACUAREMBO   TELEFONO: 4 - 20 - 94

Imprenta UNIVERSAL, Maldonado 811

Cover of *Birobidyán,* an informational brochure about the J.A.R. published in Uruguay, 1950. The Yiddish writing encourages investment in the Jewish People's Bank of Uruguay.

plague the area. In the immediate postwar years, the shortage of skilled labor hindered economic reconstruction. Officials made concerted efforts to recruit workers with job qualifications that suited the specific needs of particular industrial enterprises and collective and state farms. More important, the region was unprepared for the influx of new settlers, who placed enormous strains on the resources and infrastructure. The housing stock and roads were in a sorry state: apartments required repair, trash was strewn all over the countryside, roads and bridges needed to be fixed and repaved, and new apartments had to be built.

It is a testament to the poor quality of Soviet construction methods and materials that conditions had deteriorated to such an extent in a region where most buildings and roads were no more than ten years old. The library that had opened in 1934 was in such disrepair that it had to be shut during the winter because of a broken boiler. Water pipes leaked and the roof was also in bad shape, as was the building's facade. Overall, efforts to put things in order before the settlers arrived foundered as a result of mismanagement, inefficiency, and material shortages.

In a replay of events from the first years of settlement, the newly arrived inhabitants often found themselves living in squalor, without adequate housing, social services, and work. On several collective farms hosting new families, not all inhabitants had dishes, pots, and pans. Without sufficient beds, mattresses, and other furniture, it was common for the new arrivals to sleep on the floor. Not surprisingly, many of the people who came to the J.A.R. in these years chose to leave and look for greener pastures elsewhere. In 1946 as many as nine thousand of the fourteen thousand persons (including many former residents of the J.A.R.) who had arrived in Birobidzhan city after demobilization moved to other parts of the Soviet Union.

THE BLACK YEARS   The revival of the J.A.R. came to an abrupt halt by the end of 1948. Fearful of the perceived political disloyalty of Soviet Jewry once the state of Israel had been created, and motivated by unrestrained anti-Semitism, in 1948 Stalin launched a murderous campaign to destroy all Jewish intellectual and cultural activity throughout the Soviet Union. His ruthless attacks on "rootless cosmopolitans" and "bourgeois nationalists" culminated in early 1953 with the infamous Doctors' Plot. Numerous prominent Jewish doctors were accused of plotting the murder of leading party officials. A rumor circulated that Soviet Jews were to be sent to Kazakhstan, Siberia, and the Far East, including the J.A.R. Barracks to house the deported Jews were reportedly built, but Stalin's death in 1953 prevented the implementation of this sinister plan.

In the J.A.R. itself, leading Jewish party and government officials, along with the Jewish cultural elite, were arrested for "bourgeois nationalism" and "rootless cosmopolitanism," the two accusations most frequently lodged against Soviet Jews during the last years of Stalin's life. The Kremlin claimed that they had betrayed the interests of the Soviet people, because ties between the J.A.R. and AMBIJAN facilitated the dissemination of pro-American sentiments among the residents of the J.A.R. By accepting relief packages from abroad and asking for even more assistance from AMBIJAN, the leadership of the J.A.R. intimated that the Soviet Union required outside help and thereby fueled anti-Soviet propaganda in the West. Thus, Bakhmutskii and his assistants were guilty of "anti-patriotic conduct" and insulting "the honor and worth of the Soviet people" because their actions gave the impression that the United States and not the Soviet people were responsible for the achievements of the J.A.R.[45] Bakhmutskii was stripped of his party post and arrested for a variety of "gross political mistakes in the ideological, economic, and cultural spheres."[46] Among his misdeeds were the suggestion that the J.A.R. be elevated to the status of an autonomous republic and the promotion of Yiddish schools and publications, even though an appropriate basis for these institutions, namely a readership and student body desiring to attend Yiddish schools, did not exist.

As elsewhere in the Soviet Union, Jewish intellectuals in the J.A.R. were attacked as "lackeys of Western bourgeois culture." Boris Miller, whose play *He Is From Birobidzhan* was criticized for its Jewish "nationalist limitations," was accused along with other Jewish dramatists of being "divorced from the Soviet present" and writing about the J.A.R. as if it were the only place in the Soviet Union where Jews could flourish. The poem "My Province" by Israel Emiot was attacked on ideological grounds because "national motives dominate over the theme of Soviet patriotism of all peoples." And an article by Ber Slutskii about cultural life in the J.A.R. was condemned for mentioning only the works of Jewish writers in the library and neglecting to publicize the "classics of Marxism-Leninism, Russian literature, and Soviet writers" also housed there.[47] In sum, these writers and Bakhmutskii neglected to underscore the positive features of Jewish life throughout the Soviet Union and erroneously depicted the building of the J.A.R. with "only the hands of Jews."[48]

Boris (Buzi) Miller served as editor of the *Birobidzhaner shtern* for many years and was known for his plays. Along with other Jewish literary figures in the J.A.R., he was accused of being a "bourgeois nationalist" and "rootless cosmopolitan." He was arrested in 1949 and languished in the gulag until his release in 1956.

Miller wrote this poem on a postcard in 1954 in response to a child's letter. In the poem, entitled "A View of the Kremlin," Miller reaffirms his faith in Communism.

Dear Beloved children!
Without superfluous and unnecessary words
I've heard in your holiday greeting
the sincere call of your hearts . . .
We won't torture ourselves day and night
for we shall be separated for a short time.

The sight of the bright Kremlin
is a guarantee of this.

Ironically, these "enemies of the people" were condemned for fostering Jewish culture in a region populated mostly by non-Jews. Evidently, these artists were guilty of taking the aim of the J.A.R. too seriously and failing to pay sufficient attention to the achievements of non-Jewish Soviet citizens. Bakhmutskii understood all too well that he was being sacrificed as a result of policy shifts in the Kremlin. As he stated in defense of his actions, "I didn't understand that what is said at one time cannot be said mechanistically at another time."[49] And so he and the Jewish intellectual and cultural elite of the J.A.R. fell victim to Stalin's secret police. They had no way of knowing that their efforts to promote the J.A.R. and Yiddish culture, which enjoyed official sanction right after the war, would become political liabilities as the Cold War intensified and Stalin turned against Soviet Jewry. These artists and thinkers paid for their "crimes" with imprisonment and sometimes death.

All contact between non-Soviet Jewry and the Jews of the J.A.R. halted, and the region retreated into a period of enforced isolation. The Jewish Theater was closed, instruction in Yiddish in the schools was again forbidden, and the synagogue shut its doors and then burned down in 1956 after a fire broke out in an adjacent factory. The secret police arrested the staff of the *Birobidzhaner shtern*. (A new staff, however, continued to publish the newspaper.) The Kremlin dismantled the Jewish division of the museum, and in perhaps the most tragic action, local officials burned some thirty thousand books from the Judaica collection of the public library. In 1994 Efim Kudish, a resident of the J.A.R. since 1946, recalled the book burning and how he risked his life by concealing dozens of Yiddish books under his clothes in the library and taking them home for safekeeping.[50]

The anti-Jewish assault of Stalin's last years delivered a mortal blow to the Birobidzhan experiment. As Basya Spivak, a Soviet Jew from Ukraine, noted facetiously about the J.A.R., "I only know that the climate is terrible there. Yes. They have chosen the best place for the Jews . . . Birobidzhan."[51] Such sentiments were shared by most Soviet Jews in the post-Stalinist era who considered the Soviet Zion a hoax, if not a downright joke.

The region could never become a center of Jewish culture and life in the absence of a Jewish press, theater, schools, and intellectual and cultural activists. Jewish migration to the J.A.R. was once again suspended, though the government offered non-Jews who moved to collective farms in the region free transportation and a host of other inducements such as cash payments, tax incentives, and low-interest loans. Those Jews who did remain were terrified to express their Jewishness. The J.A.R. would never recover.

Whatever promise the J.A.R. held in the minds of both foreign and Soviet

Jews had evaporated by the time of Stalin's death in 1953. No serious observer believed that the J.A.R. even remotely embodied the national-cultural aspirations of Soviet Jewry. As Boris Miller, who survived his years in the gulag, wrote, "the Jewish Autonomous Region did not fulfill our hopes; it became instead a factory for Jewish assimilation."[52] This was precisely what the Kremlin desired.

THE POST-
STALIN YEARS

The post-Stalin era brought no substantial changes to the J.A.R. After Stalin's death, news about the region began to trickle out to Western journalists and diplomats, some

of whom visited Birobidzhan. The American journalist Harrison Salisbury, who went to the area in 1954, wrote that "it was plain that Birobidzhan had lost its significance as a Jewish centre a long time ago. . . . I could not see that the place had any special Jewish character. . . . [I]t was dead as a Jewish centre and never had had too much vitality."[53] It was clear to all commentators, including high-ranking Soviets, that Jewish life and culture had no future in the J.A.R., notwithstanding official pronouncements about the Jewish nature of the region. Even Nikita Khrushchev admitted to an Italian journalist in 1958 that "the Jewish settlement in Birobidzhan was a failure."[54] In 1959 Jews constituted just under 9 percent (14,269) of the J.A.R.'s total population of 162,856, and in 1970 the percentage had dropped to just under 7 percent (11,452). Nonetheless, it served the Kremlin's purposes to retain the region's formal status, presumably as proof of the regime's commitment to allow Jews national and cultural rights.

The sterility of Jewish life was remarkable. There were very few visible manifestations of Yiddish culture. A few street signs in Yiddish remained in Birobidzhan city, but in general, the process of Russification continued unabated since all education and government business was conducted in Russian and the government stifled any genuine stirrings of Jewish culture. The newspaper *Birobidzhaner shtern* lacked any serious Jewish content and was essentially a translation of the local Russian-language daily. In the regional museum no mention was ever made about Jewish culture, Yiddish, or the Jewish contribution to the founding of the J.A.R.

Beginning in the mid-1960s, the Kremlin, seeking to score propaganda points in the international arena, cautiously allowed the revival of Jewish cultural activity in the J.A.R. Radio performances of Yiddish songs and plays became a regular form of entertainment. Some religious activities continued. Even

Scene from the play *Mazel Tov*, performed by the Jewish Theater, mid-1960s.

Playbill of two Sholom Aleichem plays, *Doktor* and *Mazel Tov*, performed by the Jewish Theater in 1966.

though the synagogue had not been rebuilt after its destruction in 1956, some Jews continued to meet as a *minyan* in a wooden shack a few doors down from where the synagogue had stood. In addition, a ritual slaughterer had joined Solomon Kaplun, the cantor from the days of the synagogue. A Jewish theater troupe performing in Yiddish was reestablished, even though now it was composed of amateurs. Residents of the J.A.R. welcomed the revival of the theater, which they remembered with fondness and pride. Speaking about the Jewish Theater that had been closed during the repressions of the late 1940s, Rosa Kurtz, a member of the Moscow Jewish Theater that toured the J.A.R. in the early 1970s, noted, "it was evident that the theater which existed there formerly, the one that had been closed left a deep mark."[55] And in the late 1970s the Jewish Chamber Music Theater was formed, which soon moved to Moscow. Like the theater, the music ensemble spent most of its time touring the Soviet Union.

THE J.A.R. TODAY | The fact that the J.A.R. had retained its official
status for fifty years prepared the ground for the
revival of Jewish life with the ascendance to power of Mikhail Gorbachev in
the mid-1980s. The Kremlin's efforts to stamp out manifestations of Jewish culture and identity in the region were, for the most part, successful, particularly
among Jews born after 1945. Yet a framework existed in which Jews in the region could work to recover their dormant sense of Jewishness. The advent of
perestroika and *glasnost'* in the mid-1980s and the subsequent collapse of the
Soviet Union encouraged local officials and Jewish activists to revive Jewish life
in the J.A.R. They took seriously the region's status as a Jewish territory, despite
the dwindling number of Jews (in 1989 just under 9,000 of the J.A.R.'s 214,000
residents were officially classified as Jews) and the moribund nature of the Jewish community.

The desire to resuscitate Yiddish culture in the region was rooted in pride as
well as in a political strategy designed to safeguard the region's autonomous
standing. Local officials hoped to parlay this status into economic benefits for
the J.A.R. through trade and tourism. Indeed, in 1990 the USSR Council of
Ministers tried to revive Jewish settlement in the J.A.R. by offering financial
and housing assistance to newcomers.

During the first half of the 1990s, Yiddish was again offered as an optional
subject in several Birobidzhan schools, and in 1990 Yiddish and Jewish literature became part of the curriculum at the Birobidzhan Teachers' College for
several years. In the late 1980s Jewish activists established a Sunday school; in
early 1992 some 150 children and teenagers (not all Jewish) attended classes in

Today's visitors to Birobidzhan
are greeted at the train station
with both Russian and Yiddish
spellings of the city name. The
use of Yiddish on government
buildings and offices reflects the
status of Yiddish as an official
language of the J.A.R., notwithstanding the hollowness of the
region's claim to be the national
homeland of Russian Jews.

Yiddish, Hebrew, and Jewish history and culture. Several students stated that they studied Yiddish because it was their "native language" and deserved to be kept alive.[56] As of 1996 a state-supported Jewish day school and two Sunday schools were in operation. In addition, a variety of formal and informal Jewish organizations sprang up in the early 1990s, ranging from a "Maccabee Sports Club" to a Zionist youth group. The synagogue, reopened in 1984 to commemorate the fiftieth anniversary of the J.A.R., has been used primarily by a group of Seventh Day Adventists, but it is also home to a small but growing congregation of young Jews interested in Judaism. Yet plans to build a Jewish cultural center to house a Judaica library and a new synagogue were still unrealized in 1996, with little hope that the needed funds and other material assistance were forthcoming.

Contact between the Jews of the J.A.R. and various Jewish communal and academic institutions in Israel and the United States has promoted knowledge of Judaism and Jewish culture, history, and literature among the inhabitants of the J.A.R. Jewish summer camps and educational courses have been the primary vehicles. In 1994 an Israeli rabbi spent several months in Birobidzhan trying to broaden local Jews' understanding of Judaism and Jewish customs and rituals. Public celebrations of Jewish holidays such as Purim have become commonplace; in 1992 officials in Birobidzhan used municipal funds to organize a Purim celebration that was broadcast on local television, and the weekly lighting of the Sabbath candles was also televised as of 1994. Regional authorities in the mid-1990s set up a Department of Jewish Culture to stimulate the development of Jewish life, particularly the celebration of Jewish holidays, in the J.A.R. The department has also sent several students to a Moscow yeshiva in the hope of fostering Jewish culture and Judaism in the J.A.R.

Z. L. Bel'man teaching Yiddish at a Jewish Sunday school in Birobidzhan, early 1990s.

The synagogue was reestablished
as part of the J.A.R.'s fiftieth
anniversary celebration in 1984.
Jews and Seventh-Day Adventists
share it for religious activities.

In the early 1990s authorities in the J.A.R. commissioned a sculpture in the shape of a menorah to grace the grounds outside the new philharmonic hall.

Since the late 1980s Jewish life in the J.A.R. has experienced the same efflorescence of activism and commitment witnessed throughout the lands of the former Soviet Union. More than seventy years of Communist rule were not enough to extinguish all forms of Jewish self-identity, either individually or collectively. Like Jews elsewhere in the former Soviet Union, most Jews in the J.A.R. feel isolated from their Jewish heritage, Judaism being largely irrelevant to their sense of Jewishness. Yet this alienation has been broken down by a process of self-discovery that has led to a renaissance of Jewish culture, traditions, and even religion. As several experts on contemporary Jewry in the former Soviet Union write, "to be Jewish means to feel oneself a part of the Jewish people, to have Jewish parents, and to be proud of one's Jewish identity. Thus, for most Russian Jews, Jewishness is a compound of subjective feelings, attachment, biology, and pride."[57] The linguistic and territorial components of national identity, as posited by policy makers in the 1920s and 1930s, are less important than other bases of Jewish identity.

Jewish religious life resurfaced in the early 1990s, particularly during the major holidays. Public celebrations of Jewish holidays such as Purim are commonplace and receive public funding. By the mid-1990s the local television station broadcast the weekly lighting of the Sabbath candles and celebrations of other Jewish holidays.

Passover seder, 1994. The Russian letters on the prayer book spell "Pesach" (Passover).

Purim *spiel* (play), 1994.

Rosh Hashanah celebration, 1994.

Nevertheless, serious pragmatic and political obstacles hinder the resurgence of Jewish life. As in the 1930s, the lack of human and material resources jeopardize the development of a vibrant Jewish culture. Few Jews familiar with Judaism and Yiddish are still alive. While the 1989 census reveals that 1,037 Jews living in the J.A.R. listed Yiddish as their mother tongue, the number possessing mastery of the language was lower. Moreover, the steady exodus of Jews from the region diminishes the prospects of revitalizing a Jewish community. Ironically, many of the Jews departing the J.A.R. in recent years have gone to Israel, the successor state to Palestine. This, of course, was the other major Jewish utopian project of the twentieth century, demonized by proponents of the Birobidzhan project. The rate at which Jews are leaving the J.A.R. is threatening to erase the Jewish presence in the region. During the first five months of 1996, nearly nine hundred Jews, or about one-fifth of the J.A.R.'s Jewish population, left for Israel, leaving behind an ever-dwindling number of Jews who make up less than half the Jewish population of the late 1980s. The material and social problems confronting the Jews of the J.A.R. associated with this exodus are similar to those being experienced by Jews elsewhere in Russia, where emigration has also led to a steady decline in the number of Jews.

What is the future of a putative Jewish territory with a steadily declining Jewish population? There is no sign that the official designation of the J.A.R. will be taken away. Nor is there any indication that the remaining Jews of the J.A.R., no matter how small, will lose interest in recovering their Jewish heritage. Yet the state of affairs in 1996 strongly suggests that the future of Jewish life in the region is bleak, with the effort to rebuild Jewish culture promising at the very least to be an uphill struggle. Notwithstanding the positive turn of events since the collapse of the Soviet Union, the hopes and aspirations that so many of the pioneer Jews placed in the Birobidzhan experiment still have not been fulfilled.

1. The phrase was coined by Stalin. See Solomon Schwarz, *The Jews in the Soviet Union* (Syracuse, N.Y.: Syracuse University Press, 1951), pp. 38–39.

2. Quoted in Zvi Gitelman, *Jewish Nationality and Soviet Politics: The Jewish Sections of the CPSU, 1917–1930* (Princeton, N.J.: Princeton University Press, 1972), pp. 416–417.

3. *Tribuna evreiskoi sovetskoi obshchestvennosti,* (Tribune of the Jewish Soviet Community) October 1, 1928, p. 1.

4. For these quotations see, respectively, A. Fabrikant, "Agrikul'turnye cherty evreiskogo zemledeliia v SSSR" (Agricultural Traits of Jewish Farming in the USSR), *Evreiskii krest'ianin* (Jewish Peasant) 1 (1925): 24; *Tribuna evreiskoi sovetskoi obshchestvennosti,* September 1, 1928, p. 21; and State Archive of the Jewish Autonomous Region, *fond* 3, *opis'* 1, *delo* 13, pp. 4–5.

5. Viktor Fink, "Birobidzhan," *Sovetskoe stroitel'stvo* (Soviet Construction) (May 1930): 117–123.

6. V. Bugayenko, *People I Know in Birobijan* (Moscow: Novosti Press Agency, 1975), pp. 28–29.

7. *Birobidzhanskaia zvezda* (Birobidzhan Star) August 26, 1935.

8. S. D., "Evreiskaia avtonomnaia oblast'—detische oktiabr'skoi revoliutsii" (The Jewish Autonomous Region—Offspring of the October Revolution) *Revoliutsiia i natsional'nosti* (Revolution and Nationality) 6, no. 52 (June 1934): 21.

9. Interview with Bradley Berman, May 1996.

10. Lion Feikhtvanger, *Moskva 1937: Otchet o poezdke dlia moikh druzei* (Moscow, 1937: Report on the Journey for My Friends) (Moscow: Goslitizdat, 1937), p. 71.

11. Interview with Bradley Berman, May 1996.

12. Lord Marley, *Birobidzhan as I Saw It* (New York: ICOR, 1935), p. 2.

13. Gennady Estraikh, "Yiddish Language Conference Aborted," *East European Jewish Affairs* 25, no. 2 (Winter 1995): 92.

14. In those areas where approximately 4,500 Koreans lived in the J.A.R., government documents had to be published in Russian and Korean; on a collective farm inhabited primarily by Ukrainian settlers, some publications appeared in both Ukrainian and Yiddish.

15. A. Khashin, "*Forpost,* zhurnal Evreiskoi avtonomnoioblasti" (*Outpost:* Journal of the Jewish Autonomous Region) *Tribuna evreiskoi sovetskoi ohshchestvennosti,* no. 2 (223) (1937): 12–13.

16. *Tribuna evreiskoi sovetskoi obshchestvennosti,* no. 2 (128) (1932): 16.

17. Sh. Klitenik, "Evreiskii teatr na Dal'nem Vostoke" (Jewish Theater in the Far East), *Tribuna evreiskoi sovetskoi obshchestvennosti,* no. 14 (235) 1937, pp. 10–12.

18. Sh. Klitenik, "Literatura o Birobidzhane" (Literature about Birobidzhan), *Tribuna evreiskoi sovetskoi obshchestvennosti*, no. 22 (219) (1936): 31–32.

19. Gitelman, *Jewish Nationality and Soviet Politics*, pp. 339–340 and 350.

20. Interview with Nina Sirotina (p. 19) in the Oral Histories of Recent Soviet Émigrés in America Project of the William E. Wiener Oral History Library of the American Jewish Committee, now housed in the Jewish Division of the New York Public Library.

21. Interview with author, March 1992.

22. Interview with author, October 1994.

23. *Birobidzhanskaia zvezda*, February 12 and March 5, 1931. In addition, see also articles in the April 22, 1932, and September 9, 1934, issues, which also discuss the problems of Great Power chauvinism and anti-Semitism.

24. Ibid., February 12, 1931.

25. Ibid., March 5, 1931.

26. Ibid., February 27 and April 21, 1935.

27. Ibid., May 29, 1937.

28. In his monograph about Soviet policy toward the Nivkhi, an indigenous people of Sakhalin Island, Bruce Grant observes that "statist efforts at culture creation are diminished by their artificiality." Bruce Grant, *In the Soviet House of Culture: A Century of Perestroikas* (Princeton, N.J.: Princeton University Press, 1995), pp. xii–xiii.

29. Lucy Dawidowicz, *From That Place and Time: A Memoir, 1938–1947* (New York: W. W. Norton and Company, 1989), p. 100.

30. Hayim Greenberg, "Why Not Biro-Bidjan?" In *Jewish Frontier Anthology, 1934–1944* (New York: Jewish Frontier Association, 1945), pp. 32–33.

31. Itsik Fefer in the fall of 1948 responding to an article in the American Yiddish daily, *Forverts* (Forward), critical of the J.A.R. From Benjamin Pinkus, ed., *The Soviet Government and the Jews, 1948–1967: A Documented Study* (Cambridge: Cambridge University Press, 1984), p. 377.

32. Quoted in J. M. Budish, "Birobidzhan—The Jewish Autonomous Region of the U.S.S.R." *American Review on the Soviet Union* 9 no. 2 (1948): 56–57.

33. Bugayenko, *People I Know in Birobijan*, pp. 62–63.

34. *Birobidzhanskaia zvezda*, May 25, 1946.

35. In 1946 a Jewish doctor who taught anatomy at a medical institute in the Crimea stated that qualified Jewish doctors were being passed over in preference to Russians. When he complained to the institute's director about this hiring practice, the latter reportedly stated that "Jews now have to go to Birobidzhan for work." See Rossiiskii tsentr khraneniia i izucheniia dokumentov noveishei istorii (Russian Center for the Preservation and Study of Documents of Recent History), *fond* 17, *opis'* 125, *delo* 405, pp. 21–22.

36. *Birobidzhanskaia zvezda*, July 1 and 4, 1947.

37. Rossiiskii tsentr khraneniia i izucheniia dokumentov noveishei istorii, *fond* 17, *opis'* 46, *delo* 2666, pp. 186–189.

38. Ibid., *fond* 17, *opis'* 118, *delo* 428, p. 86.

39. Ibid., *fond* 17, *opis'* 47, *delo* 2680, p. 144.

40. *Birobidzhanskaia zvezda*, July 10, 1946.

41. Yehoshua Gilboa, *The Black Years of Soviet Jewry, 1939–1953* (Boston: Little, Brown and Company, 1971), chap. 3.

42. *Birobidzhanskaia zvezda*, May 17, 1947.

43. Rossiiskii tsentr khraneniia i izucheniia dokumentov noveishei istorii, *fond* 17, *opis'*, 49, *delo* 2999, p. 141.

44. Ibid., *fond* 17, *opis'*, 48, *delo* 2741, pp. 186–187.

45. Ibid., *fond* 17, *opis'* 49, *delo* 2999, p. 10.

46. Ibid., *fond* 17, *opis'* 49, *delo* 3003, p. 87.

47. *Birobidzhanskaia zvezda*, April 15, 1949. See also Rossiiskii tsentr khraneniia i izucheniia dokumentov noveishei istorii, *fond* 17, *opis'* 48, *delo* 2741; *opis'* 49, *delo* 2999; *opis'* 118, *delo* 428 for the internal party discussion of these matters.

48. Ibid., *fond* 17, *opis'* 118, *delo* 428, p. 29.

49. Ibid., *fond* 17, *opis'*, 49, *delo* 2999, p. 152.

50. Interview with author, October 1994.

51. See interview with Basya Spivak (p. 60) in the Oral Histories of Recent Soviet Émigrés in America Project of the William E. Wiener Oral History Library of the American Jewish Committee, now housed in the Jewish Division of the New York Public Library.

52. Gennadi Kostyrchenko, *Out of the Red Shadows: Anti-Semitism in Stalin's Russia. From the Secret Archives of the Former Soviet Union* (Amherst, N.Y.: Prometheus Books, 1995), p. 152.

53. Quoted in Pinkus, *The Soviet Government and the Jews,* pp. 379–381.

54. Quoted in Pinkus, *The Soviet Government and the Jews,* pp. 61–63.

55. Interview with Rosa Kurtz (p. 70) in Oral Histories of Recent Soviet Émigrés in America Project of the William E. Wiener Oral History Library of the American Jewish Committee, now housed in the Jewish Division of the New York Public Library.

56. Robert Weinberg, "Stalin's Forgotten Israel: Birobidzhan Experiences Jewish Cultural Renaissance," *East European Jewish Affairs* 22, no. 2 (Winter 1992): 42.

57. Valery Chervyakov, Zvi Gitelman, and Vladimir Shapiro, "Jewish Identity in Post-Communist Russia," *Bulletin: The Newsletter of the Susan and David Wilstein Institute of Jewish Policy Studies* (Fall 1995): 8.

SELECTED

Bibliography

The number of primary and secondary source materials in Russian and Yiddish on the Jewish Autonomous Region is substantial, with the bulk of it appearing in the 1920s and 1930s. Rather than provide a full listing, I suggest that the reader interested in exploring the history of the Birobidzhan experiment in greater depth refer to the footnotes in the text and the references used by the authors of the following works.

Abramsky, Chimen. "The Biro-Bidzhan Project, 1927–1959." In *The Jews in the Soviet Union since 1917*, edited by Lionel Kochan, 3d ed., pp. 64–77. Oxford: Oxford University Press, 1978.

Emiot, Israel. *The Birobidzhan Affair: A Yiddish Writer in Siberia*. Philadelphia: The Jewish Publication Society of America, 1981.

Gilboa, Yehoshua. *The Black Years of Soviet Jewry, 1939–1953*. Boston: Little, Brown and Company, 1971.

Gitelman, Zvi. *A Century of Ambivalence: The Jews of Russia and the Soviet Union, 1881 to the Present*. New York: Schocken Books, 1988.

———. *Jewish Nationality and Soviet Politics: The Jewish Sections of the CPSU, 1917–1930*. Princeton, N.J.: Princeton University Press, 1972.

Kagedan, Allan Laine. *Soviet Zion: The Quest for a Russian Jewish Homeland*. New York: St. Martin's Press, 1994.

Kostyrchenko, Gennadi. *Out of the Red Shadows: Anti-Semitism in Stalin's Russia. From the Secret Archives of the Former Soviet Union*. Amherst, N.Y.: Prometheus Books, 1995.

Levavi, Yaacov (Babitsky). *Ha-hityashvut ha-yehudit be-Birobijan* (The Jewish Colonization in Birobidzhan). Jerusalem: Ha-hevra ha-historit ha-yisraelit, 1965.

Levin, Nora. *The Jews in the Soviet Union since 1917*. 2 vols. London: I. B. Tauris and Co. Ltd., 1990.

Mintz, Mattityahu. "The Birobidzhan Idea: When Was It First Proposed?" *Jews in Eastern Europe* 1, no. 26 (Spring 1995): 5–10.

Pinkus, Benjamin. *The Jews of the Soviet Union: The History of a National Minority*. Cambridge: Cambridge University Press, 1988.

———, ed. *The Soviet Government and the Jews, 1948–1967: A Documented Study*. Cambridge: Cambridge University Press, 1984.

Schwarz, Solomon. *The Jews in the Soviet Union*. Syracuse, N.Y.: Syracuse University Press, 1951.

———. "Birobidzhan. An Experiment in Jewish Colonization." In *Russian Jewry, 1917–1967*, edited by Jacob Frumkin et al., pp. 342–345. London: Thomas Yoseloff Publisher, 1969.

Waiserman, David. *Kak eto bylo?* (What Was It Like?). Birobidzhan, 1993.

Weinberg, Robert. "Jewish Revival in Birobidzhan in the Mirror of *Birobidzhanskaia zvezda, 1946–1949.*" *East European Jewish Affairs* 26, no. 1 (Winter 1996): 35–53.

———. "Jews into Peasants? Solving the Jewish Question in Birobidzhan." In *Jews and Jewish Life in Russia and the Soviet Union,* edited by Yaacov R'oi, pp. 87–102. Essex, England: Frank Cass & Co. Ltd., 1995.

———. "Purge and Politics in the Periphery: Birobidzhan in 1937." *Slavic Review* 52, no. 1 (Spring 1993): 13–27.

———. "Stalin's Forgotten Israel: Birobidzhan Experiences Jewish Cultural Renaissance." *East European Jewish Affairs* 22, no. 2 (Winter 1992): 39–46.

PHOTOGRAPHIC CREDITS

Bradley Berman, © 1994: 87, 90

Birobidzhan State Television: 91

Norman Gershman, © 1984: 89

Beth Hatefutsoth. The Nahum Goldmann Museum of the Jewish Diaspora, Tel Aviv: 51

Historical Museum of the Jewish Autonomous Region, Birobidzhan, Russia: xiii–xvi, 12, 14, 24–27, 29–30, 32–33, 39 top–42, 50 top, 60–62, 66, 68, 70, 73, 75–76, 83, 86, 88

Judah L. Magnes Museum, Berkeley, Calif.: 20, 79 right

Mapmaker, Bill Nelson: 15, 17

National Center for Jewish Film, Brandeis University, Waltham, Mass.: 34 top

Productive Arts, Brooklyn Heights, Ohio: 34 bottom–39 bottom

Collection Howard Schickler Fine Art, New York: 44–49

Dia Winogrand, Santa Fe, N.M.: 50 bottom

Archives, YIVO Institute for Jewish Research, New York: 16, 19, 23, 28, 79 top left and bottom left

Library, YIVO Institute for Jewish Research, New York: xi, 22, 52 bottom left and bottom right–59, 63 (Bund Collection), 74, 78, 80–81

Collection Sanford L. Ziff Jewish Museum of Florida, Home of MOSAIC, Miami Beach: 52 top

DESIGNER   Nola Burger

COMPOSITOR   Integrated Composition Systems

TEXT   12.25/13.75 Walbaum

DISPLAY   East Bloc, DIN Neuzeit Grotesk, Gill Sans Light

PRINTER   Malloy Lithographing, Inc.

BINDER   C. J. Krehbiel Co.